Ralf Meier

# PILATES
## *Improve Your Well-Being*

edited by Heide Ecker-Rosendahl

Meyer & Meyer Sport

Original title: Pilates – Körperübungen zum Wohlfühlen
© 2005 by Meyer & Meyer Verlag
Translated by Heather Ross

British Library Cataloguing in Publication Data
A catalogue record for this book is available from the British Library

Pilates – Improve Your Well-Being
– Oxford: Meyer und Meyer, 2006
ISBN 10: 1-84126-175-0
ISBN 13: 978-1-84126-175-1

© 2006 by Meyer & Meyer Sport (UK) Ltd.
Aachen, Adelaide, Auckland, Budapest, Graz, Johannesburg,
New York, Olten (CH), Oxford, Singapore, Toronto
Member of the World
Sports Publishers' Association (WSPA)
www.w-s-p-a.org
Project Management: Johannes Ebert, txt, Bonn
Editorial (Text/Image): Alexandra Minisdorfer,
Traute Schürmann-Baetzel, txt, Bonn
Printed and bound by: TZ Verlag, Germany
ISBN 10: 1-84126-175-0
ISBN 13: 978-1-84126-175-1
E-Mail: verlag@m-m-sports.com
www.m-m-sports.com

# Foreword

In our productivity-obsessed society, there is little room for individual needs, so it is no wonder that more and more people are affected by chronic stress at work and in their professional lives.

This book is intended to encourage you to develop a more relaxed lifestyle. The Pilates method enables you to give your body, mind, and soul the attention they deserve.

Joseph Pilates was born in Germany and emigrated to America, where he published his holistic training program in the 1920s. However, it took a very long time for his effective exercise program to gain popularity in Germany. A few years ago, Pilates finally returned to the homeland of its creator, where it has since won over more and more devotees.

*Have fun exercising!*

*Heide Ecker-Rosendahl*
*Olympic champion,*
*Munich 1972*

# Contents

# The Six Elements of Pilates

More than 600 muscles keep our bodies moving. We need a few to blink and others to chew. When we feel chilly, tiny muscles contract that make the fine hairs on our bodies stand on end. Even our blood is pumped through our vascular system by small muscles.

However, muscles can be stunted by one-sided or incorrect movements. Pilates is an effective way of reeducating even the most neglected of muscles. These exercises require a special breathing technique and always work many muscles, thereby producing a muscular balance. Pilates doesn't only improve strength and endurance though, it also increases flexibility and coordination.

# An Effective Training Method for Body and Mind

**Joseph Pilates was born in 1880 near Düsseldorf and his childhood was overshadowed by illness. He suffered from asthma, bronchitis, rheumatic fever and was extremely slight. Pilates fought determinedly against his condition and began to improve his physical shape by practicing various sports. He soon developed from a sickly child into an enthusiastic athlete: Pilates took up boxing and gymnastics and, for a long while, was a circus performer.**

*Joseph Pilates in his studio training with opera singer Roberta Peters (1951)*

Over time, Joseph Pilates developed his own whole-body training program, based largely on Eastern methods/exercises like yoga. He refined his method in Great Britain, where he was imprisoned to an internment camp during World War I. With simple aids, such as bed springs, he stopped his body from declining during imprisonment. Inspired by the success of his method, Pilates later constructed special equipment with which even bed-ridden patients could carry out his exercises successfully.

When the war was over, and after a short trip back to Germany, Pilates eventually emigrated to the USA, where he opened his first studio in the 1920s. At first, the new whole-body exercise attracted mostly dancers. Pilates helped their battered bodies to recover.

Famous actors were also among the first Pilates devotees. Recently, Pilates has attracted numerous Hollywood greats and music stars, including Madonna, Brad Pitt, Jodie Foster and Richard Gere.

After the death of Joseph Pilates in 1967, his wife took over the studio and later handed it over to one of the master's former students.

*For many years, Pilates was a well-kept secret of dancers and actors. Only recently have the advantages of this whole-body training method been discovered by the general public.*

## The Principles of the Pilates Method

Pilates is a whole-body training program. The efficiency of the movements depends on several factors that all influence and build on each other.

The six most important elements of Pilates training are:

- Total movement control
- Complete concentration on the engaged muscles
- Accurate movement execution
- Gentle movement
- Emphasis on the "girdle of strength"
- Deep, deliberate breathing

Mental concentration on the body gives an enormous boost to the physical processes. However, many people find it almost impossible to concentrate on a certain muscle. Why? Because in everyday life, we usually notice our muscles if they hurt from sitting or standing for a long time. We don't have a real relationship with our muscles any longer.

To understand this more easily, it helps to take a look at how the muscles work. They receive the command to contract from the central nervous system. The more frequent the commands, the better the body's own data highway works. Frequent, deliberate contraction of a muscle accelerates this effect.

During the 1960s, there were several masters of muscle control, who were able, for example, to make wave movements with their abdominal muscles. Today, many people find it difficult to perform a deliberate muscle contraction. Just try to contract the back of your thigh without any external resistance. Not so easy is it?

## No Rest for Your Muscles!

The only ways a muscle can work is to contract or to pull together. Without the help of its antagonist, a contracted muscle will never recover from its position. The biceps illustrates this very well. It contracts if the forearm is bent. Taking the forearm back to its starting position then makes the triceps at the back of the arm contract. The stretching of the biceps muscle is therefore just the "side effect" of the triceps contraction.

Ideally, the strength ratio between a muscle and its antagonist should be balanced. Only then can we be sure that the forces that our bodies are subject to from the natural basic tension of the musculature do not cause any damage. Our modern lifestyles have an increasing tendency to unbalance this ideal ratio. This is caused just as much by one-sided loading at work and in our leisure activities as it is by the lack of physical activity that affects so many children and young people.

The damage this causes is not immediately noticeable. Damage to intervertebral disks and joint arthroses develop for many years before they become extremely noticeable painful. The initial warning signals – tense muscles, a slight pull here and there – are usually harmless and give no indication of the possible future consequences. However, this is precisely the time when

*A few muscle groups act like player and opponent: While the biceps flexes the arm, it is straightened by the contraction of the triceps.*

we should start to take better care of our bodies. Not with a passive, easy lifestyle though, but with an active exercise program.

## Performance Control

To structure training as effectively as possible and to see the first positive changes quickly, you must constantly check your movement patterns. This is why it is best to learn Pilates from qualified, experienced instructors, who can provide continual movement correction in the first phase, when the beginner's body awareness is very well developed.

*Pilates can influence and eventually improve the coordination between body, mind and soul.*

However, in Pilates, checking does not just mean relying on someone else's expert help. From the first training session, you should not just rely on the instructor, but perform every exercise in a careful, controlled manner.

At the end of the day, it is your body. No instructor, however well-trained, can know exactly what you are feeling in each muscle or joint. So be aware of any information that your body sends you during each exercise.

## MEDICAL TIP

Pilates is not just an ideal way to stay healthy, it also has a beneficial effect on existing problems of the movement apparatus. It is especially useful for all who suffer from back pain. However, always be careful in your choice of exercise!

Can you feel the difference if you bring your shoulders a couple of centimeters forward or backward? Which one feels better? Are there parts of the movement that are particularly uncomfortable? When does the discomfort start, and when does it stop? Does it increase if you change the movement slightly?

Pilates training forces you to take the initiative yourself. The instructor can only give you the initial push and serve as a competent contact while you take full responsibility for your body during every exercise.

*The shoulder bridge strengthens the back, buttocks and legs. This exercise must be performed in a careful, controlled manner.*

## Concentration

Up to now, you have possibly only been aware of your muscles in extreme situations, e.g., when shoveling snow in winter or when you last moved house. People rarely even notice their muscles during normal everyday movements.

Elite athletes are especially aware of their muscles that they can perform complex movement patterns "on dry land." Just watch a luge racer before the start: he rehearses the race physically, as well as mentally. In real time, he senses his muscles as they engage in the same sequence as they will be deployed through the race.

*As well as strengthening muscles, over time Pilates also helps to develop a differentiated physcial awareness.*

Slight body movements can even appear in these visualization exercises, also known as ideomotor actions. Studies show that mental concentration on physical movements actually improves performance considerably. That is not a license to just train while lounging on the couch though, for even the strongest concentration is no substitute for actual physical activity.

## Accuracy

The Pilates system consists of several hundred exercises, which are not all separate and equal, instead they run into each other to form routines. For beginners, there are special "pre-exercises" that should be carried out first in order to be able to perform the Pilates exercises correctly later.

*Even difficult exercises like the Side Bend must be carried out correctly from the start to avoid injury or improper posture.*

The reason behind this is a process called coordination ability, in which all the muscles engaged in a movement learn how they can work together to achieve their objective. To begin with, the movement will look clumsy, but with enough practice, it soon will look right/fluid. The learning process is only finished when the movement can be performed correctly under different conditions. The new movement will be stored as a pattern in the brain and from then on can be reproduced at will. In the later stages of the learning process, we don't need to think about the movement any longer, it will have become automatic.

## TRAINING TIP

You need patience before a new movement becomes automatic. If you have little previous sporting experience, you should not rush anything. A comprehensive activity like Pilates is a long-term investment.

Our brains do not continually have to think about our movements. However, the storage of incorrect movements is problematic because over time, these incorrect movement patterns can cause as much damage as a muscular imbalance. As most people these days do little exercise, they no longer have the necessary body awareness to sense how they should "feel", a new movement is being performed correctly.

*As movement quality is very important in Pilates, beginners in particular should only do a few repetitions so that every exercise can really be performed correctly.*

Unfortunately, it is not uncommon for incorrect movement patterns to be stored and reproduced again and again.

## THE SIX ELEMENTS

It is therefore extremely important to perform the Pilates exercises correctly from the first training session on. Incorrect movements from the earliest sessions become noticeable later on when you train at a more advanced level.

It takes a very long time to change stored movement patterns, so it is better to make sure that the movements are correct right from the start.

## TRAINING TIP

**Before you start to train, think about exactly what you what to achieve. Discuss your wishes and objectives with the instructor. The Pilates exercises are only the means to an end. You can only gain the success you want if you understand exactly why you are doing each movement at every stage.**

## Fluent Movement Performance

*Since Joseph Pilates passed away, his method has undergone constant development. Over time, different emphases have been formed, such as special rehabilitation programs.*

Although in many Pilates exercises you do exercises against resistance, it is not a form of strength training. You do not need to use centrifugal force in order to overcome the "dead point" in a movement. In powerful, explosive movements there is also an increased risk of injury. A good level of fitness and a basic warm-up can definitely reduce this risk, but it can never be completely eliminated. Never forget that you do Pilates to become healthy and more physically resilient. At every point of the movement, there is a conscious relationship between your body and your mind.

Your body should flow rhythmically during the movement. Unlike yoga or stretching, in most Pilates exercises there is no stopping point, just a slow, continual motion. The end of the movement is reached only when you return to the starting position.

With time you will have a greater range of movement for each exercise. Your muscles will become more supple and stronger. They experience the success of your continued efforts.

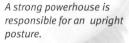

*A strong powerhouse is responsible for an upright posture.*

## The Core

In Pilates, the term "the core" refers to the abdominal area, the lower back and the gluteal muscles. Joseph Pilates called this muscular triangle that is responsible for stabilizing the lumbar vertebrae the "powerhouse." All exercises start from here. It is the center both for strength and rest. The systematic strengthening of this area is the highest priority.

The idea is that a strong core will protect the body muscles from one-sided loads, which cannot be completely avoided in everyday life. Whoever has to spend several hours a day in front of a computer or in the car in the course of his job, cannot kepp his spine in good shape. A way must therefore be found to keep the spine healthy and flexible despite one-sided loading for a whole lifetime if possible.

*Pilates exercises strengthen stretched muscles.*

Joseph Pilates was ahead of his time in this respect. Since then, more and more doctors and sports scientists have developed a controlled strengthening program for the abdominal, back extension and gluteal muscles in order to more effectively fight the new epidemic of back pain.

## Regular Breathing

Deep breathing is exactly the opposite of what we do every day. Most people's unconscious breathing technique is anything but ideal. It is too shallow and too quick, and, as such, is an expression of our hectic lifestyles. This shallow breathing makes us even more nervous and stressed. Our breathing and our emotional life are directly related and influence each other. Does the person you are talking to feel secure or is he anxious? Just take a look at his breathing and you will see. If his chest rises quickly then he feels anything but comfortable. But if he breathes slowly from the pit of his stomach, then he is completely relaxed.

*Breathing is a deciding factor in Pilates. Try to become more aware of your breathing process.*

Just as external influences make us anxious or calm, our breathing influences us. Our emotions therefore react to breathing that is permanently rapid and shallow. We feel as we breathe.

## *TRAINING TIP*

Look for a Pilates instructor you can trust. Take time to make your choice, for in Pilates you must be open and give a lot of yourself. This can't happen if you don't like your instructor. Most gyms offer Pilates courses, as do private instructors.

The next time you are at a red light or a closed cupboard and are in danger of losing your temper, do a little test: breathe deeply in and even more deeply out. Repeat this process two or three times. You will be surprised to see that your mounting anger has disappeared. This happens without too much effort. It is impossible to breathe deeply and be angry at the same time. Relaxation automatically follows deep exhalation.

It goes without saying that breathing is particularly important in a holistic  training form like Pilates. You must be aware of your breathing process to be able to focus on your negative breathing patterns and correcting them.

*Breathing is fundamental in every Pilates exercise. It improves blood circulation and aids relaxation.*

This sounds easy in theory, but it is a little more difficult in practice, as an incorrect breathing pattern is just as difficult to change as an incorrect movement pattern. It is true that practice makes perfect!

# EXERCISES

The following exercises illustrate the six Pilates elements. They are graded according to difficulty as follows: easy ( ◉ ), medium ( ◉ ◉ ) and difficult ( ◉ ◉ ◉ ).

**The Hundred** ◉

(1) This exercise is suitable as a introduction to Pilates for beginners. L on your back on a mat, with your spir in its natural "S" shape. Straighten yo arms and lay them next to your body an press the palms of your hands agains the floor. Now bend your knees and pu them toward your upper bod

(2) By deliberately contractin your powerhouse muscle slowly raise your head an shoulders slightly. At the sam time, also raise your arms fro the floor. Now raise and lowe your arms slightly and do no let them touch the floor.

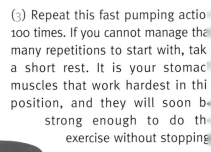

(3) Repeat this fast pumping actio 100 times. If you cannot manage tha many repetitions to start with, tak a short rest. It is your stomac muscles that work hardest in thi position, and they will soon b strong enough to do th exercise without stopping

(1) Lie on your side on the mat and activate your powerhouse by pulling your navel toward your spine. Move your feet slightly forward keeping your legs straight. Support your head on your lower hand, and put the other hand on the mat in front of your upper body.

(2) Raise your upper leg and make five to ten small circles first in one direction and then the other.

(3) Feel your gluteal muscles contract as you do the exercise. Then lower your leg back to the floor. Change sides and repeat the exercise with the other leg.

(1) Sit down on the mat with a straight spine and your legs slightly apart. Your bodyweight is over your coccyx and the soles of your feet are touching each other. Grip your ankles from inside. Do not round your shoulders.

(2) Straighten your legs and place your feet shoulder-width apart. Move your hands to the back of your thighs, which should remain straight, as should your spine.

(3) Round your back and breathing in, roll your upper body backward down your whole spine.

(4) As soon as only your shoulders are touching the mat, breathe out and start to roll back to the starting position. Repeat this rolling movement five to ten times.

1

(1) Lie down on your stomach with your legs straight and extend your arms forward shoulder-width apart. Look down at the floor.

2

(2) While breathing out, raise both the left leg and the right arm about 20-30 cm. from the floor. Raise your head slightly too and keep it in line with your spine.

3

(3) Repeat the movement with the other side: i.e., raise the right leg and the left arm. Carry out this exercise quickly ten times.

## PILATES FOR BACK PAIN

90% of people have suffered from back pain at least once in their lives. For some, it is a one-time experience, while for others it is the start of years of suffering. It is true that most victims are middle-aged or older, but more and more children and young people are being affected by this new epidemic.

Only in exceptional cases, e.g., after accidents, can the exact cause of the pain be determined. It is often not possible to establish the cause at all. The patient then begins an odyssey to different doctors at the end of which they are usually left feeling that no one can help them.

There are usually many factors involved when back pain starts. Regular sitting or standing for hours on end has an equally negative effect, as do lifting heavy objects, the cold – especially draughts – and genetics. Even mental problems can affect back pain. If several factors come together, the local metabolic processes can become unbalanced.

Many sufferers of back pain find that the affected area feels colder than the rest of the back a few days before an attack. Judicious Pilates training can rebalance the local metabolic functions and is therefore an effective aid in the fight against back pain.

## SUMMARY

- Pilates trains the body, mind and soul.

- The Pilates method is based on the six principles of checking, concentration, accuracy, fluent movement, centering and breathing.

- Only an active person can take control of his own destiny.

- From beginner to top athletes, Pilates is suitable for every level.

# Starting to Work Out

We are all getting older, and those who want to remain active in their old age need the right amount of exercise. In our technological world, sport has become an indispensable compensation for our chronic lack of activity. But not every form of activity does this in the desired way, as many sports are very one-sided and end up overloading the body instead of healing/ improving it.

# The Different Forms of Pilates

**Pilates ceased to be an obscure exercise form a long time ago. From being just a well-kept secret among dancers and actors, it has since developed into a popular training method that is now taught in nearly every gym. As the system has evolved continually since the death of Joseph Pilates, there are now several variations and styles.**

The variety of Pilates classes available can be rather confusing for beginners. The basic distinction is between classes that use equipment and those that use mats. Most gyms only offer classes using mats, while specialist Pilates studios also use equipment.

Along with the classic apparatus "the Reformer", a whole arsenal of equipment has now sprung up. The almost endless number of exercises and exercise variations can also be confusing for the beginner.

*The training equipment developed by Joseph Pilates should make the exercises easier. The best known piece of Pilates equipment is the Reformer, a bench equipped with pulleys, spring resistance and a sliding carriage tracking system.*

It is not really important which type of Pilates you choose to practice. The core elements of the system are the same whichever you choose. There is one thing that you should watch out for though: many instructors and course leaders teach a particular form of Pilates that they specialized in during their training.

The basic and intermediate courses that you attend afterward should always be in the same Pilates style. Do this until you can justifiably call yourself an advanced Pilates student. When you are a beginner, and the movements are not yet that familiar, mixing Pilates methods can slow your progress.

For experienced students, the opposite is true. It does them good from time to time to broaden their horizons and enrich their training with different equipment and new exercises.

Over time, it may even be a good idea for you to select a few exercises from different Pilates methods to suit your individual needs and lifestyle, thus creating a brand new form of Pilates.

## Developing Your Body Awareness

One of the most attractive things about Pilates is the great scope for creativity that it allows. Before you enter this experimental stage though, you must know your body very well and above all be able to really communicate with your muscles.

### TRAINING TIP

If you intend to enroll for a Pilates course, you should ask if you can participate in or attend a trial session. In Pilates, you have to express yourself and this can only happen in an environment where you feel comfortable and with people you like.

You have to invest a lot of time in basic training until you reach this level. This naturally depends on your condition when you take up Pilates. Very few people have a well-developed body awareness when they start Pilates. There may be muscles or muscle groups that you find easier to build up contact with at the start, and others that you can hardly feel and find it hard or impossible to contract. Those people who can communicate well with their bodies have usually done a lot of sport before. They already know that the smooth interaction of nerves and muscles is vital for body awareness, and that is just a question of training.

It takes time for your muscles and nerves to work together. This is particularly true in the case of Pilates, which is not about training individual muscles, as it is in the case of general fitness training, but about training complex muscle groups.

The more muscles engaged in a movement, the harder it is to coordinate them and make them work together. Beginners in particular who have never practiced sports in their lives before, and who are attracted to Pilates by the apparently easy, flowing exercises, should realize that they will need patience as well as interest. Not everyone can immediately master the exercises as well as a trained dancer, who, because of her previous training, can usually get a feel for a movement just from a description of it.

*In line with the Pilates Principle, the basic "Double Leg Stretch" exercise engages several muscles.*

The connection between nerves and muscles can not only be improved by Pilates exercises. You can also do isometric exercises anytime and anywhere, i.e., tensing your muscles without even moving. You should do this particularly with muscles and muscle groups with which you do not have a very good connection already.

## The First Steps

Don't be deceived by the fact that Pilates looks easy at first sight. Compared to many other training methods, Pilates is definitely one of the most demanding.

If you have not practiced any sports for a long time, it would be wise to start some recreational activity before your first Pilates class so as to regain some body awareness. Ball games are admirably suited for this, as they use many different muscle groups. If you would prefer, you can slip on your old roller skates or go ice-skating.

*Like yoga, Pilates features a close connection between breathing and movement.*

You can then feel immediately whether your muscles are working well together or not, or whether your movements are as flowing as they used to be. You can also go walking or jogging, although these activities engage fewer muscles and are rather one-sided.

Just as you should do before you start any new sport, make sure you have a medical check-up before beginning your Pilates course.

You should realize from the outset that there is no single training method that can make you forget the consequences of a sedentary lifestyle overnight. The body enjoys any kind of exercise, as that it what it is intended to do. After many years of inactivity, our muscles completely forget what they are supposed to do. Also, we are sometimes not even strong enough to be able to perform comparatively simple movements correctly.

*A simple, structured exercise program can help to prepare your rusty muscles and joints for Pilates.*

Muscles do not only react to exercise, they also adapt to a passive lifestyle. If they are hardly stimulated at all, they will get weaker and weaker. Many of us know what it looks like when you have broken a bone and the plaster is removed. The muscles in the affected area quickly become wasted.

In fact, it happens so quickly that the phase of complete rest is made as short as possible.

A sedentary lifestyle causes muscles to waste in exactly the same way. Of course, it does not happen as fast as it would if we rest completely after breaking a bone. It is much more gradual, so that we do not realize it is happening and it is harder and harder for us to manage tasks that require strength. When we do realize this and actually start to do something about it, we often blame our age.

This flimsy excuse is refuted by several scientific studies. Research clearly shows that with the right training, anyone can stay strong right into old age.

## Set Your Compass

As a Pilates novice who has not done any sport for years, it may be that you are not strong enough to do an exercise that the person on the next mat can do easily.

The stomach musculature in particular is often so unused that even relatively easy exercises can be very problematic in the beginning. Do not let this discourage you. Slowly but surely your strength will increase with regular practice.

*A passive lifestyle leads to gradual muscle atrophy. Avoid this by strengthening your muscles with Pilates. The "Swimming" exercise works on your gluteals, back, pelvic floor, arms and legs.*

It helps to structure your training around specific goals, but make sure they are realistic! If, in your first class, you plan to have the body awareness of your instructor as soon as possible, you will soon stop enjoying yourself. Pilates is not a miracle method to be done occasionally in your spare time, but a life's work that you can enjoy well into your old age.

*As a beginner, do not be discouraged if you cannot do some exercises like the "Double Leg Kick" straight away.*

To be able to practice Pilates that long, you need a great deal of motivation, patience and discipline. These necessary requirements do not come to you just like that. If you have not exercised for some time, it generally means that you will find it hard to stick to a regular training program. This time you have find the necessary motivation.

The first step is usually quite easy. A new sport initially offers enough variety to keep beginners hooked. Empirical evidence shows that it takes about six weeks for a new habit to form and get used to it. You must not, under no circumstances, give up training during these six weeks. You may not know if you want to continue with Pilates in the long term.

Do not start a course if you already know that you have booked your next vacation during the second half of the course. Going to class or working out at home must become an integral part of your daily life. Ideally, you should be sad to miss a canceled class instead of being happy to have the evening off.

The next step, which is briefly mentioned above, is setting small, realistic goals. The goals themselves are of secondary importance; what matters is that with a little effort they can be achieved. This ensures that you are constantly improving and always motivated. Of course, you are not going to improve dramatically in the short time before you reach your goal, but after many small successes you will not imagine at all that you could fail to achieve your next objective. You will see that nothing succeeds like success.

*Pilates helps to give you new body awareness and a vibrant, self-confident radiance.*

## TRAINING TIP

**Although Pilates is a gentle training method, you should still warm up thoroughly before the exercises. Activities that use a high proportion of muscle mass are best suited for this. A short endurance training session is ideal. Do not overdo it though, for you could be burning up energy in the warm-up that you will need later in your Pilates class.**

# Exercises

The following exercises give an idea of the diversity of the Pilates System. They are graded according to difficulty – easy (◉), medium (◉◉) and difficult (◉◉◉).

### Arm Circles Against the Wall ◉

Stand up straight with your back against a wall. Look straight ahead, extend your neck upward, pull your shoulder blades downward and inward, and press your spine against the wall. Your feet should form a V shape (heels touching).

While you breathe in deeply, raise your straightened arms in front of your body until they are parallel to the floor (1). Contract your stomach muscles. Slowly make a circle with your arms: bring them upward (2), to the side, downward (3) and then in front of you back to the starting position. Repeat this movement three times and then circle your arms in the opposite direction. Repeat this movement three times also.

### Roll Down the Wall ◉

The starting position for this exercise is the same as for Arm Circles. However, this time, let your arms hang down loosely by your sides and relax your fingers (1). Now start to roll downward. First, lower your head forward, then your shoulders (2), while pulling your navel toward your spine. Tilt your pelvis slightly and pull your pubic bone up. As you roll down, try to feel every vertebra as it bends forward following your head. Your lumbar spine should remain pressed against the wall.

When you have finished rolling down, circle your relaxed arms loosely three times outward and then three times inward (3), then straighten up again vertebra by vertebra until you have reached the starting position. Repeat the exercise twice.

## The Swan ● ● ●

**1**

(1) "The Swan" is a ve
demanding Pilates exercis
that requires very good boc
awareness. Start by lying c
your stomach and place th
palms of your hands flat o
the mat below your shoulder

(2) Activate your back muscles
and straighten your arms while
breathing out

**2**

(3) Bring your arms forward and roll forward
along your upper body, while swinging your
straightened legs upward and keeping your feet
together.

**3**

(4) Lower your legs again, whil
simultaneously raising your uppe
body. Keep your body tensio
throughout the rocking movement
Repeat the exercise five times.

**4**

(1) Lie on your side on the mat. Support your head on your lower hand, your other hand is placed on the floor in front of your body and helps to keep balance. Activate your powerhouse and bend your legs slightly forward from the hips.

(2) Raise both legs together with your heels touching until the upper leg forms a horizontal line with your hips.

(3) Raise and lower your lower leg, keeping the upper leg level with your hips. Breathe in as you raise and breathe out as you lower. Repeat the exercise up to ten times without touching the floor with your lower leg. Finally, bring the legs back to the floor and repeat the exercise on the other side.

## CAN YOU LEARN PILATES BY YOURSELF?

There are two essential things to remember when learning Pilates without professional instruction, which most students need much time and practice to acquire: a good body awareness and a deep understanding for the characteristics of each exercise. If these two pre-conditions exist, it is possible to train by yourself.

However, for most people, it is still advisable to take at least the first steps with expert guidance. Practically nobody would think of learning yoga or tai chi alone, for all the benefits of these disciplines would be lost. A good instructor can see immediately whether or not the exercises are performed correctly.

Without the practiced eye of a trainer, it is extremely difficult to spot and correct small errors of posture or execution. That is even more true if you do not have any practical experience of the movement yourself. In addition, mistakes that can creep in and eventually become ingrained are very difficult to eradicate later.

So, it is much more sensible to at least start learning Pilates in a class, for example, in a good gym with trained Pilates instructors. There are so many of these around that you are sure to be able to find a class that suits you.

## SUMMARY

- Every kind of sport – including Pilates – is an invaluable way of compensating for the chronic lack of exercise.

- Do not let yourself be confused by the number of Pilates variations.

- Learn to communicate with your muscles.

- Slowly get your body used to regular exercise.

- Your muscles react to activity, as well as to passivity.

# The Pilates Powerhouse

No area of our body is as badly neglected in our daily lives as our "middle": the muscles that connect the diaphragm and the pelvis. It is usually only after a bout of lumbago or some other complaint that limits our movement and results in an expanding waistline that we realize how much this part of our body affects our well-being. A strong core stabilizes the pelvis and takes the pressure off the back, thus forming an important basis both for static postures and dynamic movements. The gentle but effective Pilates exercises specifically strengthen this important part of the body.

# The Targeted Strengthening of the Center of the Body

Joseph Pilates called the center of the body the powerhouse. The term shows how important this area of the body is. Well-trained stomach and gluteal muscles and strong back muscles form the basis of an upright yet flexible posture. By strengthening the powerhouse, Pilates helps avoid problems like back pain.

*Pilates exercises strengthen the muscles around the spine.*

As we have already seen, there are many causes of back ache. It is also true that the pain often bears no relation to the seriousness of the damage. Many people whose spine is overloaded feel well, whereas others can hardly get out of bed even though it may turn out that they are only suffering from muscular tension.

Apart from the stomach, there is no other area of the body where the close connection between mind and body is so needed.

Mechanical overloading, as well as chronic stress or mental problems, can trigger bad back aches. Chronic spinal pain eventually becomes a stress factor in itself that severely diminishes quality of life.

A significant goal of Pilates training is therefore being able to recognize and interpret the signals that our body sends us. Which needs – possibly long-neglected – does my body have, especially my back? What can I do to meet these needs? Back aches in particular are often the result of one-sided loading. A few muscles are constantly overloaded, while others are hardly used at all. Pilates exercises are intended to correct these muscular imbalances.

─────── *TRAINING TIP* ───────

If you do Pilates at home, you should buy an exercise mat from a specialist sports shop. The floor is too hard for your spine, even if you train on a carpet. Even a blanket doesn't absorb the pressure nearly as well as a suitable exercise mat.

It is usually the shoulder-neck area and the lower back that are affected by the negative consequences of one-sided loading. The stunting of the lower back muscles is particularly dangerous, as they are important for the stability of the whole trunk and also for the Pilates powerhouse.

*The spine functions as a unit. If a problem occurs in one part, e.g., the lower back, then the whole system can no longer function properly.*

## Between Loading and Relaxation

Although degenerative changes to the vertebral bodies and to the spinous and transverse processes can also cause back pain, the most common problems affect the intervertebral disks. These are more than just elastic springs between the vertebral bodies, and can actually be considered to be independent joints.

The 10 to 20 fiber rings around the jelly-like core of the intervertebral disks, the so-called nucleus pulposus, can move in different directions, which allows the core to bend forward, backward and sideways and also to perform rotational movements.

The disks are composed of mucopolysaccharides and a large amount of water. The fluid content varies between 70 and 90% depending on age and physical condition and has a major influence on how the intervertebral disks function.

The fluid provides high pressure inside the disk, enabling it to withstand strong external forces. When we lift weights, they shrink by several centimeters under the load. At the end of the load, they resume their former shape and size.

## MEDICAL TIP

Don't wait until you have back problems to start strengthening your powerhouse. Don't let things get to that stage. Regular Pilates training gives you a level of vitality and zest for life that you may not be able to imagine today.

So that the intervertebral disks can do their job well for as long as possible, they need a regular supply of fluids and nutrients. Unlike muscles, the disks are not part of the vascular system that normally transports nutrients. They therefore rely on two other means of supply. Nutrients and metabolic products travel directly through the cell walls by diffusion. But this method of nutrient supply is very ineffective and delicate compared to that of the blood supply.

The second method is the pumping action produced by regular loading and relaxing. The pumping action eliminates water from the disks and takes up new liquid and nutrients.

The disks therefore require not only movement and pressure but also rest phases so that they can fill themselves with fluid. Our busy lifestyles make these rest periods rare. We sit for hours in front of computers, in the car or in front of the TV, making it impossible for the disks to assimilate sufficient fluid and nutrients.

Sitting is not a pleasant experience for our backs. Worse still, muscles and ligaments adapt to the sitting position, so that the pelvis tilts further and further backward and over time becomes completely static.

*A very effective Pilates exercise for strengthening the back is the "Leg Pull Back" (see page 133), in which straightened legs are alternately raised in line with the torso, held for a short time and then lowered back to the floor.*

**The main causes of back pain are lack of exercise, postural damage, obesity and stress.**

As with any sporting activity, you should not do Pilates either on an empty or a full stomach. Try to eat at least two hours before working out, ideally consuming a high proportion of complex carbohydrates (wholegrain, vegetables).

That is why many occupational doctors have suggested the restructuring of the work place for years. They suggest getting rid of one-sided procedures, and instead implementing flexibility and movement. What is to stop us from answering the phone standing up or scheduling a short exercise break every hour? It will not reduce productivity and will probably even raise it. Nobody works better with tensed back muscles!

*In order to relax your disks, you should get into the habit of stretching your back regularly during sedentary activities. "Dynamic sitting" is also a good idea, i.e., sitting on an ergonomic stool or a Swiss ball. You can also try to do some work standing up.*

In addition, we should take into consideration that the body's posture depends on complete muscle chains and not on individual muscles. If only the back extensor muscle is properly trained, it cannot ensure the most economical posture by itself. This depends on its interaction with other muscles in our core. Many Pilates exercises are therefore very complex movements that engage many different muscles and thus enable the modern "sedentary man" to gradually experience better body awareness.

## A Sixpack is Not Enough

While many people's back muscles are tensed, their stomach muscles usually lead a stunted existence. Though there are "spare tires" around many waists, many people's dream would be a washboard stomach. The sought-after "sixpack" is formed by a single slab of muscle laced with tendons. It is true that the rectus abdominis muscle greatly contributes to our physical appearance, but it is just one part of the abdominal muscle group. The lateral abdominals also have an important job to do, and they should not be neglected either.

Unfortunately, very few people have sufficiently developed abdominal muscles, and even people with a low body fat ratio have a little pot belly. This means that the abdominal musculature is too weak to withstand the pressure from the organs behind the abdomen. This not only an aesthetic problem; the abdominal musculature is also a protective wall for the sensitive muscles of the abdominal cavity. How weak the abdominal muscles are on average can be seen by the difficulties many people have standing up from a lying position. Strong abdominal muscles require neither lateral support not the full recruitment of the pelvic musculature to reach a standing position.

Dr. Axel Gottlob, a biomechanics expert and former elite athlete, sets out further advantages of strong abdominals in the table on the next page.

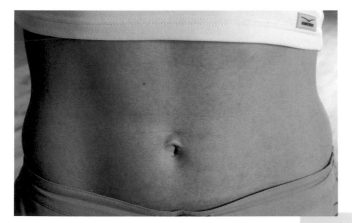

*Pilates trains mainly the deep abdominal muscles that are very weak in most people.*

# The Advantages of Functionally Trained Abdominal Muscles

Increased trunk stability and functionality.

Improved performance and effective injury prevention for all athletes.

The arms and legs can be positioned faster and more soundly in highly dynamic activities, such as throwing, punching and kicking.

Improved coordination.

Increased spinal relaxation by:
- Increasing horizontal traction over the lumbar-dorsal tissue
- Improving braking and returning ability from maximal positions.

Beneficial influence on the body posture as a whole with positive psychological effects.

Improved flexibility of the lumbar spine and the middle/lower thoracic vertebrae.

Improved protection of the whole abdomen.

Physiological organ massage that stimulates the digestion.

Relevant pressure/alternating load for the vertebral joints, vertebral bodies and disks for the purpose of improved diet and increased strength.

Improved figure due to a slimmer waist.

A strong lateral "abdominal muscle corset" gives a natural-shaped waist and a strong abdominal musculature and low body fat produce the famous "sixpack."

# The Importance of the Gluteal Muscles

Along with the back and abdominal muscles, the large gluteal muscle, the gluteus maximus, is also particularly important for the powerhouse. It is mainly involved in the positioning of the pelvis and therefore also the lumbar spine. The gluteal muscles are often neglected. A well-trained and well-shaped bottom is actually even more sought-after than a sixpack, but just as rare. This is true for both men and women. It does not matter how big the bottom is, the muscle below the fatty layer is usually small and weak. Well-trained gluteals play a vital role in avoiding and combating back pain.

*Regular Pilates training strengthens the gluteal muscles, which are an important component of the powerhouse.*

## Lost Body Awareness

We have seen that most people must start to train for a strong powerhouse very gradually, as the area that is so important for their health and well-being has been so totally neglected. This is also due to our modern lifestyles that alienate us more and more from our bodies. We must therefore ask a coach or a doctor which movements are good for us or not, because we are no longer able to interpret what our bodies are telling us. Is a pulled muscle just a result of increased strength training, or could it be the start of a serious injury?

*Playful experimentation in childhood, e.g., climbing trees, is crucial for the development of body awareness.*

It is very strange that we have to learn something at a fairly advanced age that should be obvious. Today's adult generation only became sedentary at a late age. In their childhood and youth, they were able to run around and explore their own physical limits. It is more difficult for today's children to develop a healthy body awareness. They often only know from books that trees can be climbed. Six-foot high climbing walls therefore represent an insurmountable obstacle for many people.

Children today often lack the strength and coordination even for undemanding physical activity. It is no wonder, since they practically grow up sitting down. It starts with the circle of chairs in kindergarten and sitting at desks in high school, and continues into leisure time sitting in front of a computer for hours. The result is shocking: more and more children and young people suffer from adult onset diabetes, metabolic disorders and obesity.

As Joseph Pilates developed his training system, he could hardly have imagined how significant his principles would one day become and how important they would be even for relatively young people.

*As the name "Pilates" is not protected, many styles have sprung up that are adapted for specific people such as pregnant women or children.*

## Use Your Powerhouse

The powerhouse is much more than just a stabilizer for the lower back. Once you have gotten the muscles in this area into shape, you will see that your whole body benefits. You not only feel stronger and more energetic, but you also have more mental stamina. You remain fresh for the whole day, because tensed muscles are not only uncomfortable but also tiring. Pilates training prepares all your muscles properly for the job they have to do. At night, you will be rewarded with a restful and relaxing sleep.

Because the powerhouse has such importance for the whole body, you should always do the special exercises to strengthen it at the start of your program. Make yourself aware of the muscles in this area.

Try to communicate with them by concentrating on a certain muscle and just blocking out the rest of the body. You may not succeed right away, but you will get better at it with time. To start with, concentrate on a large muscle, e.g., the gluteus maximus. You may well be sitting on this muscle as you read this book.

## TRAINING TIP

Before you start to do the exercises, you should go through each one in your mind first. Feel your muscles before they actually move. The efficacy of the exercises increases with the ability to perform each movement sequence consciously.

First, deliberately contract your right gluteal muscles, and then the left. Next try to contract both sides together. Concentrate on what you feel. How does the muscle react? How does your sitting posture change? Try to feel as much as possible, as this will be a valuable aid in the later phases of training when you do very difficult exercises.

Pilates is not about just copying a movement that is demonstrated to you. The training method is more a way to fulfilling your needs. Perhaps you have been repressing many of these needs for years in order to deal with

*A good exercise to improve balance and body awareness is "Rolling Like a Ball" (see page 108).*

everyday stress. This kind of repression can only be superficial though. You cannot fool yourself permanently, at least not without causing some kind of damage to your mind and body.

## The Power of Your Needs

Think of how many times you have had to combat negative attitudes or emotions in the past few days or weeks. They are hiding unexpressed needs. They can be basic things like too little sleep or food, or unsatisfied emotional needs. Incidentally, repressing or deliberately ignoring such needs has nothing to do with discipline. Instead, your mind and body are showing you that you need certain things to function properly and perform well.

Imagine that you are deprived of well-deserved sleep for three days. You would not be able to do anything. You would not even be able to stand up, and you would not be able to concentrate either. This is exactly what happens if you ignore other important needs. Maybe this happens because you are just no longer aware of

*Pilates can help you to take more notice of your personal needs.*

your needs, or you can no longer interpret them correctly. The advantage of Pilates is not just that you improve your physical performance; this holistic training method also activates your inner communication.

It is up to you to decide how important each individual need is. Just accept that you have the need so that you can deal with it lucidly. This enables you to get some control over your own life and also some freedom. Emotions show you the path you should take, like a navigation system. People who trust their "gut instinct" often turn out to make better decisions that those who only follow their heads.

## TRAINING TIP

Pilates is not just a good training system in its own right, it is also a fantastic complement to other sports. The strengthening of the powerhouse has a positive effect on performance for most sports. It is no wonder then that many elite level athletes include special Pilates exercises in their training programs.

As our brains are still very young in an evolutionary context, they make many mistakes. On the other hand, our emotional nature has been developing for several million years. A large part of our behavior is genetically programmed and can therefore be invoked more quickly in times of need.

Learn to understand the answers that your gut gives you and use them in your everyday life. Pilates opens physical closets and frees the way for a journey of spiritual discovery at the end of which lies a deep feeling of security and confidence in your own abilities.

*The best advisor is always your own internal voice – you only have to know how to listen to it.*

# Exercises

The following exercises strengthen the powerhouse, among other things. They are graded according to difficulty – easy (◉), medium (◉ ◉) and difficult (◉ ◉ ◉).

## Single Leg Stretch ◉

(1) Lie on your back and raise your head and shoulders from the floor and bend one leg and pull your knee toward your chest. Keep the other leg straight and at an angle of about 45 degrees. Hold your bent leg between the knee and ankle, with the opposite hand holding your knee. Imagine that the straight leg is getting longer and longer. Avoid twisting your body by keeping your powerhouse straight.

(2) Alternate your legs without stopping: bend the straightened leg and straighten the bent leg and point it upward at a 45° angle. Repeat the exercise ten to fifteen times. To finish, pull both legs onto your chest and relax.

## Double Leg Stretch ●

(1) Start in the same position as the Single Leg Stretch, then bend both legs and pull your knees onto your chest. Lay your hands flat just above your ankles, breathing out and raising your head and shoulders from the floor as you do so. Feel how the contracting abdominal muscles pull you right away from the floor.

(2) Remove your hands and hold them out straight beside your body. Then extend both legs together until they are almost vertical and breathe in. Pull your knees back to your chest again and place your hands around your leg just above the ankles. Repeat this exercise ten to fifteen times. During the whole movement, make sure that your lower back does not lift off the floor by pulling your navel toward your spine. When you straighten your legs, you can easily hollow your back.

## Criss Cross ● ●

(1) Lie on your back on the mat with your legs bent and clasp your hands behind your head. Extend your left leg and turn your upper body to the right, bringing your left elbow toward your right knee.

1

(2) Then extend your right leg, bend your left one and pull your knee toward your chest and turn your upper body to the left. Adapt the leg changes to your breathing rhythm and repeat the whole movement three times.

2

**1**

(1) Lie on your side on the mat. Activate your powerhouse by supporting your head with your lower hand and placing your other hand on the mat. Straighten your legs and angle them forward slightly.

(2) Breathe in and raise your upper leg quickly toward your head. Feel the contraction in your glutes as you do so.

**2**

(3) Breathe out and lower your leg again, but do not let it touch your other leg. Repeat this movement five to ten times. Change sides and repeat the exercise with the other leg.

**3**

(1) Sit on the mat and bend your legs, placing your hands palms down on the floor behind you to support yourself. Your feet are flat on the floor and you should breathe calmly and regularly.

(2) Now straighten your legs as far upward as possible so that only your hands and your bottom are touching the floor. Your feet are in a V position and your toes are pointed.

(3) Make a small circle to the right with both legs, and then a small circle to the left. The upper body should remain still throughout, the back should be absolutely straight and the abdominal muscles pulled in. Repeat the whole movement sequence three times and then lower your legs.

(1) Lie on your back and raise your straight legs toward the ceiling. Stabilize your body by placing your arms on the floor by your sides.

(2) Contract your abdominal muscles and as you breathe out, carry out a double scissors movement: one leg moves forward and the other backward, then change over. Perform the scissors movement three to five times and then lower your legs onto the floor.

1

2

(3) A variation for advanced practitioners is to start from the same position as above, then using the strength of your abdominal muscles, raise your hips and roll upward until only your shoulders are touching the mat. Support your back with your hands.

(4) As you breathe out, the legs make a scissors movement back and forth. After three to five repetitions, breathe in as you roll down vertebra by vertebra back to the starting position and lower your legs back onto the floor.

3

4

**THE POWERHOUSE** — **65**

## CONCENTRATION

Most people must train to develop the concentration required to practice Pilates. Concentration means that all of one's attention is focused on a certain objective or thing. Modern psychology assumes that a great deal of concentration is dependent on a certain state of neurological excitement. Stress, anxiety or depression have a negative effect on one's state of excitement and therefore limits the ability to concentrate. You have probably already experienced that for yourself.

For example, think back to the last time you drove a car after arguing with your partner or when you were under stress at work. The pressure you were under at the time maybe meant that you could not concentrate properly on the traffic. You noticed the traffic lights changing later than normal and only spotted the brake lights of the car in front at the last moment. In short, under such conditions it might have been better to take a taxi.

At times like these it is hard to do Pilates. So change your mood at the right time. Take a few minutes' break before your Pilates class to step back from your everyday stress and get in the right mood for your class by imagining pleasant things. Imagine that you are shutting out all the unpleasant thoughts whizzing around inside your head for an hour. Instead, think of the best times of your life, like your last vacation. This will automatically give you the necessary mental relaxation required to be able to concentrate fully on your class.

## SUMMARY

- The powerhouse is formed by the abdominal, gluteal, pelvic floor and lower back muscles.

- Our spinal cord is a particularly delicate wonder of nature.

- To be able to work properly, the vertebral disks require alternate loading and relaxation.

- Trained abdominal muscles provide protection and stability.

- Strong gluteal muscles can prevent back pain.

- Good body awareness can be learned at any age.

- These days, many children lack strength and coordination.

# Beginners Program

The following exercise routine brings you the basic principles of Pilates. The Beginners Program is a combination of the exercises described in detail at the end of each chapter in this book as well as additional exercises. This training routine will help you to get to know your body better and strengthen your muscles.

(1) Stand up straight, tense your leg musculature, pull your pelvis slightly forward and upward, activate your powerhouse by "sucking" your navel toward your spine. Pull your shoulder blades together and down.

1

2

3

(2) Begin with the basic "Roll Down" exercise. Sit with a straight spine on the mat and bend your legs. Grip the backs of your knees with your hands.

(3) Pull your navel firmly toward your spine, round your back and roll across one vertebra after the other. Stop the movement as soon as you can no longer keep the soles of your feet on the mat. Try to let your hands go for a moment and then roll back upward with a flowing action. Repeat the rolling down and up five times and slowly relax.

**4**

(4) The next exercise is the "Single Leg Stretch." Lay your straightened arms on the floor beside your body and bend your legs into a right angle at the knees.

(5) Pull your right leg toward your chest, hold your right knee with both hands while extending your left leg diagonally upward and lifting your head and shoulders off the floor.

**5**

**6**

(6) Alternate your legs: bend the left leg, pull the left knee toward your chest and extend the right leg diagonally upward. During these leg changes, keep both your powerhouse and your box straight. Repeat the exercise eight times for each leg. Lie back down on the mat and relax.

(7) For the "Single Leg Circle" exercise, raise your left leg straight up. The next time you breathe in, start to circle your straight leg clockwise. Make six complete, controlled circles.

7

(8) Now, circle your left leg six times counterclockwise. Then put your leg back onto the floor.

8

(9) Now, perform the exercise with your right leg. With time, you can vary the tempo and do some circles more quickly. Always make sure your movements are controlled though.

9

(10) After a short rest lying on your back, bend your legs at right angles, draw them onto your chest and point your toes ready to perform "The Hundred." Lay your arms beside you.

10

11

(11) Lift your head and shoulders off the mat and raise your straight arms from the floor slightly. Start to "pump" your arms up and down in a rapid but controlled manner. Perform five arm movements each time you inhale and exhale. Repeat the fast pumping action 100 times. Then lie down on your back and relax.

**12**

(12) For "Rolling Like a Ball," come into the sitting position. Take your feet off the floor and either wrap your hands around your lower leg or grip the hollow of your knees.

(13) Then round your back and next time you inhale, roll backward under control. Introduce the forward rolling movement before your head touches the floor. Do this exercises five times.

**13**

**14**

(14) After a short relaxation phase, do the "Spine Stretch". Sit up straight on the mat with your legs apart. The legs do not need to be straight, it is more important that the spine is. Extend your arms forward.

(15) The next time you exhale, bend forward head first. Roll down vertebra by vertebra. As soon as you have reached the end position, slowly straighten yourself up. Repeat the rolling movement ten times and then relax.

**15**

(16) "Relaxing" concludes the exercise routine. Sit on your heels on the mat.

16

(17) Round your back and let your upper body slide onto the mat, with your forearms facing forward.

17

18

(19) Then roll your back upward vertebra by vertebra until you are sitting on your heels again. Relax for a few moments at the end of the exercise routine.

(18) Bring your arms back and place your hands beside your legs. Relax for a few breaths in this position.

19

# Breathing Makes the Difference

We need oxygen to live. Even a few minutes without oxygen leads to irreparable brain damage or even death. Breathing is the way we take in this indispensable gas. The influence of breathing on the mind and body has been known for a very long time. Asia, in particular, has seen the development of the most diverse breathing techniques.

# Gas Exchange in the Lungs and the Body Cells

Breathing consists of alternately filling the lungs with fresh, oxygen-rich air and then eliminating used, carbon dioxide-rich air. The air normally travels to the lungs via the nose. An average of ten breaths per minute is sufficient to ensure the exchange of carbon dioxide and oxygen. This requires a healthy nose with a sound mucus membrane and adequate permeability. You can see how delicate this system is when you start to get a cold. The mucus membrane swells up and blocks the flow of air so much that you have to breathe through your mouth to compensate.

*Our lungs consist of two wings. The left wing is divided into two parts and the right wing into three parts.*

Once it enters the body, the breath passes down the windpipe into the bronchial tubes. This branching system of tubes takes the air to about 500 million tiny sacs in the lungs called alveoli. As the right heart ventricle pumps carbon dioxide-rich, dark red blood into the lungs, it flows past the alveoli and absorbs oxygen and simultaneously gives up carbon dioxide. The color of the blood changes during this process: oxygen-rich blood is light red.

The newly oxygen-enriched blood travels down the pulmonary vein to the left heart ventricle, from where a powerful pumping action sends it on its way around the whole body. The oxygen in the blood is almost all bound to the red blood pigment, called hemoglobin.

The upper airways are strongly affected by the constant increase in environmental pollution and harmful chemicals. More and more people have to deal with a chronically blocked nose due to a swollen mucus membrane.

What starts out as a troublesome ailment can soon turn into a serious health problem. We automatically compensate for restricted nasal breathing by breathing through the mouth, which is only intended to be a supplementary measure in the case of high physical loading. When air enters the nose, it is moistened and warmed by the mucus membrane.

Bristly hairs also filter large dust particles from the air. None of this happens when you breathe through your mouth, and it also raises the heart rate and increases blood pressure.

## MEDICAL TIP

**Look after your mucus membrane as you do the rest of your skin, and do it regularly. Don't just think of your nose when it starts to get cold outside; start looking after it now. You will be rewarded by fewer infections and better health.**

Many people turn to decongestant drops or sprays to unblock their noses. In the case of an infection that disappears after a few days, they can be beneficial, but as a long-term medication, they cause further damage to the already damaged mucus membrane.

Especially in urban areas, many people's mucus membranes are over-irritated by central heating, exhaust gases and smog. So start taking preventive measures now. Cleansing with saline solutions is the most suitable way to do it. If your mucus membrane is very dry, you can also use an enriched nasal ointment.

## Learn to Breathe Right

From when we are born until we die, we breathe several million times to keep ourselves alive. So however natural the breathing process may be, our modern lifestyles make it much more difficult.

*The ability to breathe calmly and regularly is important because breathing affects both the cardiovascular system and the vegetative nervous system.*

Tense muscles and stressed minds can soon mean that breathing does not seem so natural at all. Air does not just flow inside us; it is sucked in and carried on its way by a complex system of muscles. To perform well at a high level requires correct breathing.

The way we breathe reflects our physical and mental condition. Instead of breathing deeply and calmly, many people's breathing is shallow and rapid. If your shoulders are rounded and your chest musculature is not developed, it is extremely difficult to inhale deeply with every breath and to squeeze as much residual air out

**MEDICAL TIP**

**Deep, relaxed breathing is also beneficial for your psyche. If stress makes your heart work overtime and the problems of this world are just too much, take a little time out. Let the air flow into your lungs and exhale deeply. After just a few deep breaths, you will feel how the pressure lifts.**

of your lungs as possible every time you exhale to make room for the next breath of fresh, oxygen-enriched air.

Before you start to work on the principles of Pilates breathing, you should familiarize yourself with your own breathing pattern. How do you breathe when you are not consciously thinking about it?

You can only find this out if you take the time to observe your breathing without trying to influence it, which is not at all easy.

You will catch yourself trying to control and change the rate or the depth of your breathing. Perhaps you will even feel panicked. Very anxious people should therefore only concentrate on their breathing under the guidance of an experienced course leader.

*Try to be aware of your breathing and the muscles engaged in the breathing process.*

## Where Does the Air Go?

Observe calmly what happens to your body as you breathe. Lie comfortably and relaxed on your exercise mat and try to block any disruptions around you. Let your breathing flow and try not to influence it. Initially, it may help if you recall a couple of happy memories to distract yourself from your own mundane thoughts.

As soon as you are really relaxed, notice how it feels when the air is drawn into your nose.

Feel how the air brushes past the tiny hairs inside your nose and flows down your throat toward your lungs. Concentrate carefully on how your thorax and abdomen change as you inhale and exhale.

*Beginners are particularly advised to do breathing exercises lying relaxed on their backs.*

You will be astonished how flexibly your chest reacts to the air that is drawn into your body with every breath. The thorax not only expands upward but also sideways. If you breathe deeply enough, you can even feel your ribs being squeezed together. Even your stomach is involved in the breathing process. It almost seems as if the air surrounds your internal organs and pushes the stomach.

However, many people's breathing is so shallow that their thorax hardly rises at all and the air flows back out again immediately. Most people lie somewhere between these two extremes.

It is true that they do not fully exploit the possibilities of their lungs, but they do not run the risk of choking due to cramps. The lungs have a great deal of room available to move that is nowhere nearly fully used, even during exercise.

 **MEDICAL TIP**

**Try not to deliberately change your breathing rhythm. You can change your position and make sure you breathe deeply during the exercise, but it is just as hard to permanently change your breathing as it is to change your heart beat. Both are controlled by your vegetative nervous system and are therefore not subject to your will power.**

The efficiency of your lungs can be determined by lung capacity tests that measure the amount of air produced during a VO2 max test. On average, the amount varies from 3-4 liters, with well-trained athletes achieving 6-7 liters.

## A Different View

In our Western philosophy, the function of the lungs is limited to their task of exchanging gases. X-rays, bronchioscopies and 3-D images have greatly demystified the breathing process. Things are seen very differently in many Eastern cultures. For a practitioner of yoga, breathing is, among other things, an important way of communicating with oneself. However, in our part of the world, our philosophy is slowly changing, so that at least

*A targeted training program can prepare you physically to breathe deeply and regularly.*

we now accept that the way we breathe reveals our physical and mental condition. It shows if we are anxious, in pain, nervous or excited.

## NUTRITIONAL TIP

**Overeating doesn't only have a negative effect on physical training, but also on our breathing. Just think of people who sit at the table breathing heavily after a big meal. If you load your stomach to the limit, your diaphragm hardly has room to move, so don't eat too much before Pilates training.**

You can influence your breathing with the power of your imagination alone. Just remember a time when you were not only anxious and afraid but really panicking. Imagine this moment as clearly as if it were really happening. Although you may be lying on your terrace in the sun, you will feel your breathing getting shallower and your pulse rate shooting up. Your physical reaction to the frightening memory differs very little from what it would be if the situation were real. Your brain does not distinguish between fantasy and reality. The more vivid and accurate your imagination, the stronger your physical reaction will be.

*When we are very stressed, our breathing is rapid and shallow. In a relaxed state, it is slow and rhythmic.*

This also works the other way around. If you are in a situation that seems worrying or threatening, thinking peaceful thoughts can help you to keep a clear head so that you can concentrate better on solving the problem.

Too much stress stops you from thinking rationally, which is where breathing can help. Deep, calm, regular breathing not only protects you against stress, it also enables you to concentrate properly.

*The special Pilates breathing technique means that you finish a class feeling strong and in a good mood.*

## Pilates Breathing

In Pilates training, you should aim to breathe deeply and calmly. It is particularly important to the thorax that you inhale and exhale as completely as possible. You can monitor both of these yourself by placing your hands on your ribs and observing whether they expand in all directions when you inhale, including laterally. When you exhale, the ribs should pull together as much as possible. At first sight this looks easier than it actually is. However, it requires a good level of fitness plus the right kind of practice to be able to inhale enough air to make your lungs expand out to the sides of the thorax.

Ideally, your body should be able to breathe deeply all by itself. But, this can only happen when the necessary conditions exist and the strength ratios of your trunk are correctly distributed.

*Pilates breathing: To check that your breathing technique is correct, place your hands on the lower ribs.*

Many people feel heaviness in their shoulder and chest muscles. But this sensation should be felt lower in the powerhouse. This is really the center of your strength.

*The diaphragm is a muscular partition wall between the thoracic and abdominal cavities. As you breathe in, it curves downward, then as you breathe out, it curves upward again, squeezing the used air out of the lungs.*

The heaviness and restriction in the chest area is the result of tense muscles, caused by sitting for hours at a desk or in the car.

If, when you start doing Pilates, you find it hard to feel the inhaled air at the side of your thorax, don't just give up! It is difficult for most sedentary workers at first. Many people suffer from tense back muscles and irritated intercostal muscles, which is what stops you from breathing correctly.

So that the lungs can expand in all directions when you breathe in, the muscles in this area must be very flexible. If this is not the case, the lungs do not have enough room to move.

Many muscles work together when you breathe in deeply. For example, for your breath to be able to enter your lungs, the diaphragm and the muscles involved in the breathing process must contract. This creates suction in the thorax and that fills the lungs with air. As we breathe out, the diaphragm relaxes and curves upward again, squeezing the used air out of the lungs.

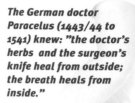

*The German doctor Paracelus (1443/44 to 1541) knew: "the doctor's herbs and the surgeon's knife heal from outside; the breath heals from inside."*

The wide back muscle is particularly important for effective exhaling. Known as the latissiums dorsi, when it is well-trained, it looks like a wing underneath the skin. This is the muscle that should be hit if someone chokes and has to be pat on the back. This external effect automatically triggers a coughing reflex that is usually enough to free the airways again.

As in all the Pilates exercises, mastering the correct breathing technique demands constant practice. Always bear in mind the following mantra: the means are the end. The more confidently you handle your body, the easier and quicker your progress will be.

Correct Pilates breathing will soon become second nature to you. For this, you need to control and also relax the important muscles involved.

 **TRAINING TIP**

**Good aerobic endurance also has a positive effect on your breathing, so don't forget to do some jogging or cycling to complement your Pilates class. You will find that Pilates training enables you to perform better in other sports and improves your overall sporting ability.**

# Exercises

The following exercises encourage you to concentrate on your breathing. They are graded according to difficulty – easy (●), medium (● ●), difficult (● ● ●)

**Relax** ●

(1) Lie on the mat on your back in the relaxation position. Then pull your knees toward your upper body with your hands and raise your head from the floor. Then rock gently forward and backward on your back.

**1**

(2) After rocking a few times, roll forward into a squat position and put your fingers on the floor to support yourself.

**2**

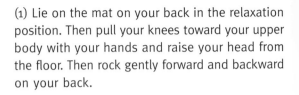

**3**

(4) The next time you breathe out, roll upward vertebra by vertebra.

(3) Straighten your legs as you exhale.

**4**

**Relaxing** ●

(1) Sit on your heels on the mat.

**1**

**2**

(2) Round your back and let your upper body slide forward onto the mat with your forearms stretched in front of you. Concentrate on your breathing and gently stretching your back muscles. Enjoy the growing feeling of relaxation.

**3**

(3) Bring your arms back and place them next to your legs. Relax in this position for a few breaths.

(4) Then roll upward vertebra by vertebra.

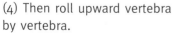

**4**

## The Saw ●●

(1) The Saw will help you to squeeze used air out of your body while also strengthening your waist and back. Sit upright with a straight spine on the mat. Press your legs down onto the mat and part them slightly. The arms are held out to the sides.

(2) Breathe in deeply and turn the right side of your body forward and the left side backward, also moving your head and keeping in line with your spine. Maintain the tension in your stomach and keep your back straight.

(3) While you breathe out, bend forward and touch your left foot with your right hand. The right rib cage is pulled diagonally toward your left hip. Your left arm points straight behind you. Do not move your hips. Hold this position briefly and then sit up straight again. Now bend to the other side. Repeat this exercise two or three times.

# The Seal ● ●

(1) Sit on the mat with your back straight. Pull your legs up and let your knees fall beside you. Hold your ankles with your hands from the inside outward so that your feet are not touching the mat and the soles of your feet are touching each other. Feel the weight of your body bearing down on your coccyx. Pull your navel in and activate your powerhouse.

**1**

**2**

(2) Round your back and roll backward while inhaling.

(3) Roll back to the starting position as you exhale. Repeat the exercise five to ten times. Make sure that you don't build up momentum with your head or your neck, but round your back so much that you can roll back and forth under control.

**3**

## MOTOR LEARNING

The term "body awareness" that is used extensively in this book is virtually synonymous with coordination ability. By this, we mean the optimal interaction of all the muscles and muscle groups that allow our bodies to move. Ideally, our muscles learn how to perform complex movements without wasting energy and damaging the passive movement apparatus in childhood. We see this so-called motor learning when we learn a new Pilates exercise, and it is divided into three phases. The first phase of gross coordination is typified by clumsy, rather awkward movements. In the second phase, fine coordination, the movement is already sufficiently stabilised that you can control the exercise by your own physical sensations. The movement cannot yet be recalled on demand, i.e., its performance is dependent upon certain standard conditions. To be able to do the exercise consistently under variable conditions, the third stage, finest coordination must have been reached. The length of time required to perform an exercise perfectly naturally depends on how difficult it is.

With regular training, you will be able to master the basic exercises very well after a few weeks. However, the Pilates system also includes movements that you will struggle with all your life. So set yourself realistic goals and only increase the level of difficulty when you are good enough at one level of performance.

## SUMMARY

- Check your breathing.

- Stress and bad posture have a negative effect on your breathing.

- Positive emotions have a beneficial effect on your breathing.

- Eastern cultures place much more importance on breathing than we do.

- Pilates breathing uses the whole thorax.

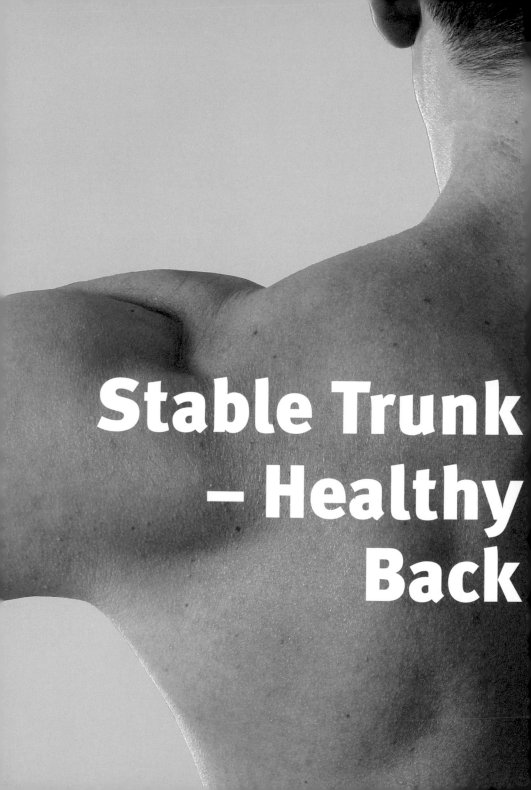

**Stable Trunk
– Healthy
Back**

Pilates exercises focus on the whole trunk, which includes the thorax and the spine, as well as the powerhouse. Joseph Pilates called the upper body "The Box." This can perhaps be more accurately described as the rectangular area formed by the shoulders and the hips. The focus on the Box is intended to align the trunk correctly at each stage of every exercise.

The connection between the Pilates Box and the powerhouse is the spine. In each exercise, attention should be paid to the position and movement of the spine. Its exact alignment also affects the all-important Pilates breathing.

# "The Box" and "The Spine": Pilates Posture

**The term "fitness" has been around for about the past 20 years, and its interpretation has changed since then. Today, it is synonymous with an attractive, sporty appearance, whose most sought-after features are toned muscles, a low body fat percentage and a year-round suntan.**

Fitness originally meant all-round physical and mental ability. However, what many people spend their leisure time doing these days is no more than just cosmetic. People want well-defined muscles without necessarily wanting to be more healthy. Standard back training with the lat pull machine and a hyperextension machine cannot correct defective posture by themselves.

First, a trainer must be found who is able to recognize defective posture and then to develop a suitable exercise program and to provide expert supervision. Very few people are lucky enough to find this though. Some trainers have at best only a basic knowledge, and they certainly don't have the time to spend working with just one client.

*A balanced fitness training program should help recovery, keep you healthy, and improve your condition.*

The original idea of strength training – by whichever means – is to strengthen the muscles so that they can do their job of moving and stabilizing each part of the body. People who train with the aim of stimulating the growth of certain muscles for aesthetic reasons have a completely different point of view. It is true that muscle size and functionality are not necessarily compatible, but they don't help each other either, especially if certain muscles are built up disproportionately purely for aesthetic reasons. This spoils the body's balance and means that some muscles are no longer able to work properly.

*The Saw is a Pilates exercise (see page 88) that forces you to focus on the alignment of the Box.*

The trunk in particular suffers from the effects of this kind of unbalanced training. In the chapter on the powerhouse (starting on page 44), we saw how abdominal muscles, back extensors and gluteal muscles together do the job of stabilizing and protecting the lumbar spine. But it is not just the powerhouse that relies on well-conditioned musculature. The part of the body that Joseph Pilates called the Box features many muscles that in most people are too weak to do their job properly. The entire spine requires the support of the surrounding musculature in order to remain pain-free and upright into old age. If this is not the case, bad posture can set in over time that can influence the static of the spine and sooner or later can lead to chronic back pain.

## Do All Sports Strengthen the Trunk?

There is no question that moderate physical activity has a positive effect on our health and our well-being. The immune and cardiovascular systems become more efficient and the muscles used benefit from the loading. However, many sports neglect the trunk musculature.

Whether football, tennis or squash, most sports feature asymmetrical, one-sided movements in which substantial forces act one-sidedly on the muscles. This one-sidedness also affects the trunk musculature.

Even jogging is not much better from the point of view of one-sidedness. Of course, running, like other endurance sports, has many positive effects on our health. However, it does very little to train the muscles of the upper body. Even if it is complemented by a couple of strength training exercises, it still lacks variety. The back musculature in particular, especially in the upper shoulder area, is so

complex that it cannot be fully strengthened with one or two exercises. Also, most exercises are never varied, they are always done in the same way, and over time both the muscles and the nervous system that is responsible for transferring impulses become accustomed to this monotony. Familiarity leads to stagnation. At a certain point, training then just maintains the status quo and the impulse for further positive adaptation is lacking.

Just lie as comfortably as possible on the floor when your back muscles feel tense. **When you stand or sit, your body posture automatically compensates to reduce the pain. This evasive posture is just the same as bad posture. The best way to establish exactly where the muscles are most sensitive to pain is to lie down. Only when you are completely sure where the pain is can you take action to deal with it.**

On the other hand, small but regular variations in the way you perform exercises lead to further improvement. And they are desperately needed to correct bad posture. Pilates training meets just these requirements, as it offers new or modified and more complex movements in every class.

The constantly changing conditions work the musculature sufficiently. These varied motor demands also lead to improved coordination ability.

## The Spine

Our backbone is a true wonder of evolution. Mother Nature really thought of everything when she constructed the spine. There is only one thing that her plan did not foresee: that we would spend most of our lives sitting down or working under other one-sided loads.

*The spine is what allows us to stay upright. It supports the head, the trunk and the upper limbs. It also protects the sensitive spinal cord.*

No other joint can compare with the spine for flexibility. The vertebral joints are responsible for providing the great range of movement to the 24 vertebrae. The cervical spine consists of seven vertebrae, the thoracic spine of twelve and the lumbar spine of five vertebrae. At the bottom, the spine terminates in the sacrum and the coccyx. This complex also represents the connection with the pelvic girdle.

## TRAINING TIP

**Imagine your spine to be a chain of pearls, of which the chain between the pearls is flexible. To maintain this flexibility, the whole spine must gradually be engaged in the movements of the Pilates exercises. Otherwise you will only train part of the spine and the rest of the spine will not benefit.**

The spine consists of vertebral bodies and vertebral arcus, which together form the spinal cord canal. This canal contains the spinal cord that runs from the brain and the spinal nerves. Between the vertebrae are the intervertebral disks, whose most important components are the rings of fiber surrounding the core (see page 47 onward).

*On every vertebral arcus, a spinal process sticks up at the back and a transverse process sticks out at the side. These processes are attached to ligaments and muscles.*

Where the nerves emerge from the protective bone marrow canal in the cervical and lumbar spine, problems with the intervertebral disks are very painful. Depending on the type and degree of damage, a so-called slipped disk can even lead to paralysis. But the precursor of a slipped disk, the protrusion of the core, is extremely unpleasant and can be accompanied by feelings of deafness.

So that it can cope with even extremely heavy loads, a healthy spine is not like a rigid tube, but has a natural curvature. In the cervical and lumbar spine, it curves forward (lordosis) while in the area of the thoracic spine it curves backward (kyphosis). At the bottom of the spine, the sacrum is shaped like a shovel. This arrangement enables the spine to absorb extremely heavy loads relatively easily, as long as it is healthy. If this is not the case, it just takes one seemingly harmless movement to cause terrible back pain.

The most frequent cause of back ache is curvature of the spine, in which the shape of the curvature is not that which nature intended. In the case of a flat back, the arci are too small, leading to reduced elasticity. A hollow back is very common, in which the lumbar lordosis is very pronounced.

The rounded back is easy to recognize; it is caused by an over-pronounced thoracic kyphosis. Lateral deviations, which are mostly due to a twisting of the vertebral bodies, are called scoliosis. Although these deviations and defective postures are not that common, they always cause pathological changes that stop the spine from working properly.

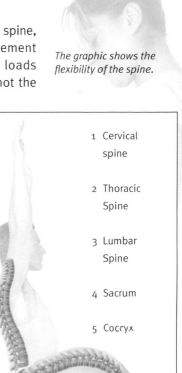

*The graphic shows the flexibility of the spine.*

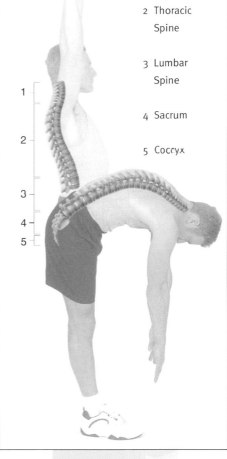

1 Cervical spine

2 Thoracic Spine

3 Lumbar Spine

4 Sacrum

5 Coccyx

## Muscles and Joints Flexibility

Whether they are to be done standing up, on a mat or using special equipment, all Pilates exercises are primarily designed to strengthen the trunk musculature. Don't forget, however strong an arm is, it can't lift a heavy load if the abdominal and back muscles are stunted by a life of physical inactivity. The strength that we can use in our everyday lives is determined by the strength of our trunk muscles. Pilates doesn't just train the muscles but also the bones, thus allowing the spine and other joints to gain long-term benefits from the exercises.

*The Pilates method features many trunk muscle strengthening exercises such as the push-up.*

Abdominal, back, chest and shoulder muscles do not just support bones and joints, including the spine, they also provide the appropriate stimuli to keep them healthy and efficient. Unfortunately, it is widely believed that it is impossible to stop our joints seizing up in old age and that we cannot stop our bone density from decreasing, and that it is our unavoidable destiny to suffer from osteoporosis.

However, joints and bones can easily continue to do their job well into old age, as long as they are not neglected. Just look at the incredible performances people can achieve if they have practiced sports sensibly all their lives. We are not talking just about elite athletes here.

*If muscles are loaded unevenly for a long time (e.g., sitting down for long periods), the muscles become hardened. Over time, they shorten and get less and less flexible.*

Instead, take as role models those people who regularly do just the right amount of exercise to keep their bones, muscles, tendons and ligaments working efficiently, that can be maintained for many years. Someone who has learned over many years to control the contractions of his muscles can still be more flexible at the age of 70 or 80 than an unfit, sedentary 20-year-old.

## TRAINING TIP

Using the full range of movement of a joint doesn't mean resembling an "India rubber man" in the circus or a world-class gymnast. These performers have become "double-jointed" as a result of years of intensive stretching. For example, an elite gymnast can move his joints well beyond the range of movement that nature intended. It certainly looks spectacular, but it has nothing to do with healthy sports. So, train moderately.

Contrary to popular belief, it is not the ability of our tendons to stretch that stops us from putting the palms of our hands on the floor when we bend over. Their flexibility is very limited and a traditional stretching program will barely improve it. Our muscles are much more stretchable.

*One-sided movements limit both our strength and our flexibility.*

Muscles exert a force on the bones via the tendons when they contract. Like all other body tissue, bones are formed of cells. The cells are nourished by mineral salts circulating in the blood. As this process is very complex, it takes a long time for any changes to take effect. However, bones do adapt to loading over time; the stimuli for this come from all the pushing and pulling demands of the muscles.

The more regular and pronounced these stimuli are, the more salts are deposited in the bones, thus increasing the bone density. So along with an adequate calcium intake, a long-term strength training program is the best protection for the passive movement apparatus and a significant step toward the prevention of osteoporosis.

## MEDICAL TIP

**Don't force it! Our civilization already creates enough pressure to achieve. So avoid giving yourself extra pressure during Pilates class by setting your expectations too high. Learn to enjoy doing the exercises and doing something good for your body, and the positive effects will come all by themselves.**

In healthy bone tissue, around 60% of the bone mass is composed of mineral salts. So that the construction processes in the bone can run properly, the body requires vitamins C and D along with calcium. While vitamin C supports the formation of the fiber protein collagen, vitamin D ensures the assimilation of ingested calcium by the intestine. Bone tissue is particular. Unlike a muscle fiber that always contracts on demand, bones only have an adaptive reaction in the area that is directly loaded. For this reason, complex movements with a continual change between high body tension and deep muscle relaxation is usual in Pilates exercises and are preferable to isolated strengthening exercises. This kind of exercise should be incorporated into your training program.

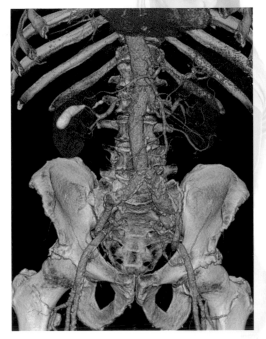

Exercises with complex movements are particularly important for people over 40, when the bones start to lose density slowly but continually. We often only associate this reduction with the broken hip so feared by old people. These breaks are usually caused by commonplace falls, require lengthy treatment and often lead to complications.

*This 3-D MRI image shows a skeleton with internal organs.*

The whole skeletal system – including the spine – is affected by this slow bone deterioration. Targeted Pilates training can stop the loss of bone matter and even reverse it over the long term. It is certain that a bone's stability depends on the strength of the musculature it is attached to.

Our joints also benefit from regular Pilates training. Joints that are not moved sufficiently become really "rusty." Only when joints are exercised through their total range of movement do the joint capsules, ligaments and

*Regular exercise stimulates the bones, thus reducing age-related loss of bone density.*

tendons receive the constructive stimuli they need to remain efficient and flexible right into old age.

## Finding Time for Pilates at Work

This chapter ends with a few suggestions as to how you can take the pressure off your back during your daily routine. In the chapter on the powerhouse, you saw that the intervertebral disks must be moved so that they can absorb fluid and work smoothly (see page 47 onward).

In some professions, we can actually decide ourselves when and how we move, but those who work long office hours do not have this privilege. A taxi driver or a traveling salesman is forced to spend much of his working life sitting behind the steering wheel. A computer operator is expected to sit staring at a computer all day and the supermarket cashier can only leave her seat during her breaks. However different these jobs may appear, the hours of sitting down they involve mean that they all are ideal breeding grounds for back pain.

 **TRAINING TIP**

If you work in a office, take a break every hour and sit up and straighten your spine. Turn your head slowly to the right and then to the left. Then bend your head forward and slightly backward. Finally, lower your head to your right and then your left shoulder. Repeat the complete routine. This simple exercise allows you to mobilize your cervical spine at any time.

Do not let yourself be discouraged by this gloomy prospect. Even if you can do little to change your working conditions, there are still a couple of easy ways to take the pressure off your back. The intervertebral disks must be allowed to rest sometimes so that a regular fluid exchange can take place. Even short bouts of relaxation go a long way toward making you feel better. You should aim for regularity, so make a little time for your back every hour. Make sure that you exercise all three parts of the spine. Sitting is most damaging for the lumbar spine, but this one-sided posture also places a lot of strain on the cervical and thoracic areas of your spine.

*Working at the computer often leads to back tension. Simple mobilization exercises help prevent back pain.*

# Exercises

The following exercises strengthen and mobilize the spine. They a
graded according to difficulty – easy (◉), medium (◉◉) and diffic
(◉◉◉).

## Roll Down ◉

(1) This basic exercise is admirably suited to practicing the controlled rolling up and down of the spine. Sit with your back straight on the mat. Activate your powerhouse, bend your legs and place the soles of your feet flat on the mat. Hold the backs of your knees firmly with your hands.

(2) Round your back and roll backward vertebra by vertebra. Stop the movement before you are no longer able to keep the soles of your feet flat on the mat.

(3) Release your hands and keep the tension. Then roll back up in one flowing movement. Repeat the exercise up to five times.

# Roll Up ●

**1**

(1) Lie on your back on the mat and stretch your arms backward.

(2) As you breathe out, raise your arms until they are vertical.

**2**

(3) Roll your upper body, head first, vertebra by vertebra upward while activating your powerhouse.

**3**

(4) Roll forward until you can touch your toes with your fingertips. Your feet should remain on the floor throughout the exercise. As you breathe out, return slowly and under control back to the starting position. Repeat the exercise five times.

**4**

## Rolling Like a Ball ●

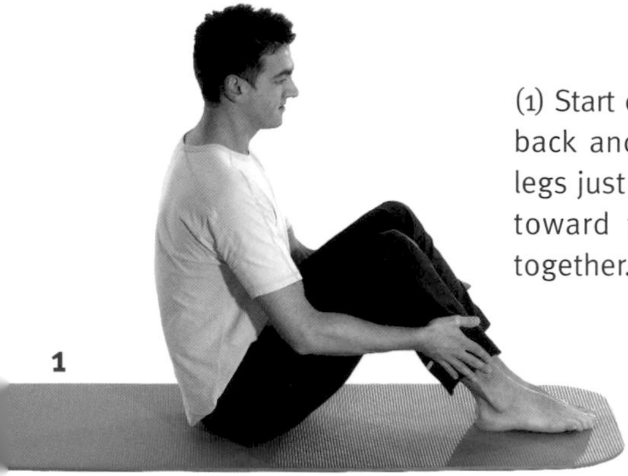

(1) Start off sitting on the mat with a straight back and your legs bent. Hold your lower legs just above your feet and pull your legs toward your bottom, keeping your feet together.

**1**

**2**

(2) Round your back and place your head between your knees and try to keep your balance in this position.

(3) Next time you breathe in, ro backward under control withou changing your body position.

**3**

(4) Before your head touches the floor, star to move back up again. As you do so, concentrate on rolling up vertebra by vertebra Make sure you roll in a straight line; don' go "off-track." Your legs should be as still as possible throughout the exercise. Repea the rocking movement up to five times.

**4**

(1) Sit up on the mat with your legs apart and stretch your arms forward horizontally.

(2) Contract your bottom muscles strongly and as you breathe out, roll your upper body slowly forward vertebra by vertebra. Round your back as you pull your stomach in.

(3) Slide your head between your outstretched arms. Unlike the traditional forward bend, the movement in the Spine Stretch is forward not downward. When you cannot go any further forward, sit up again slowly one vertebra at a time and repeat the exercise up to five times.

(1) This time, lie on your stomach on the mat. Look at the floor and contract your abdominal muscles. Place your hands on the floor under your shoulders and press down. Keep your elbows next to your body.

(2) Roll your upper body up using the strength of your back musculature. Do not push up with your arms! Pull your navel toward your spine and your shoulders down. Stretch out your cervical spine.

(3) Now, turn your head to the right as you breathe in.

(4) As you breathe out, bring your head forward again and pull your chin slowly toward your chest to stretch the muscles in the area of your cervical spine.

(5) Raise your head again, breathe in and slowly turn your head to the left. Keep the rest of your body still. Repeat this complete movement twice.

## Spine Twist

(1) Sit on the mat with your back straight and your legs stretched out in front of you. Activate your powerhouse and raise your arms to shoulder height. Feel how your spine stretches as you breathe in.

**1**

(2) As you breathe out, turn your upper body to the right, moving your arms with you. The turning movement should come from the waist. Keep your head in line with your spine and look in the direction that you turn.

**2**

**3**

(3) As you breathe in, return to the starting position and then breathe out as you turn to the left. Repeat this exercise five times on each side.

## HOW MUCH WEIGHT CAN THE SPINE SUPPORT?

It is really amazing how much loading our spines can support. A normal intervertebral disk can theoretically withstand a load of about 300kg. The biomechanics expert and sports scientist Dr Axel Gottlob has demonstrated that a man's healthy spine can support a load of one metric ton if the load comes from above. A woman's spine could support half this amount. With appropriate training, these unbelievable amounts can even be doubled.

However, the important thing is from which direction the load presses on the spine and the vertebrae. The easiest loads for our spine to cope with come directly from above. The situation is very different if the load must be supported in a posture that is uncomfortable for the spine. It the spine is twisted, it is harder to lift things. So for example, trying to lift a crate of mineral water by your side with both hands can easily end up with a trip to the osteopath. This construction that is otherwise so strong is very vulnerable in this position. This is all the more true if the spine is already damaged. Lifting heavy loads with straight legs is also far from ideal for the spine. Even many years of Pilates training cannot alter this, but at least it gives you enough body awareness to know automatically how to position your body and how to pre-tense the muscles you are going to use later to lift a load.

## SUMMARY

- Most sports load the muscles too one-sidedly.

- The spine needs the support of the surrounding musculature.

- The passive movement apparatus can also be trained with Pilates.

- The nervous system needs varied stimuli.

- Use every opportunity for Pilates training.

# Intermediate Program

As soon as you have learned the Pilates principles and gained good body control, you can start this training routine, which continues from the Basic Program (pages 68-73). The Intermediate Program is a combination of exercises that are described at the end of each chapter in this book plus some additional Pilates exercises.

(1) Activate your powerhouse by pulling your navel toward your spine.

(2) Lie on your back for the first exercise "Criss Cross." Bend your legs and bring your knees to your stomach. Clasp your hands behind your head.

(3) Stretch out your right leg, twist your upper body to the left and pull your right elbow toward your left knee. The twisting movement should only come from your abdominal muscles.

(4) Now stretch out your left leg, pull your right knee toward your chest and twist your upper body to the right. Repeat the whole sequence five times and then relax.

(5) Lie on your back to prepare for the "Double Leg Stretch." Bend your knees and place your arms beside your body.

(6) Breathe out as you pull both legs toward your chest. Place your hands on your lower legs and at the same time, raise your head and shoulders from the floor.

(7) Breathe in as you release your hands, and stretch out your arms parallel with the floor, while you stretch your legs upward. The next time you breathe out, pull your knees toward your chest again. Repeat this exercise ten times. Then relax on your back.

(8) The next exercise is called "Corkscrew." Lie on your back on the mat and raise your straightened legs vertically upward. Contract your gluteal muscles firmly so that your legs twist outward slightly and your heels touch each other and your feet point outward.

8

(9) As you breathe out, make a clockwise circular motion with your straightened legs. Pull your navel firmly toward your spine and press the palms of your hands against the floor.

9

(10) As soon as you reach the starting position, make a circle with your legs in the opposite direction. Repeat this circling movement five times in each direction and then relax.

10

1) Start "Side Kick Circles" lying on your side. Straighten your legs
nd angle them forward slightly. Support your head on your lower
m, place your other arm in front of your
dy to help with your balance.

11

(12) Contract your gluteal muscles and breathe
out as your raise your upper leg.

12

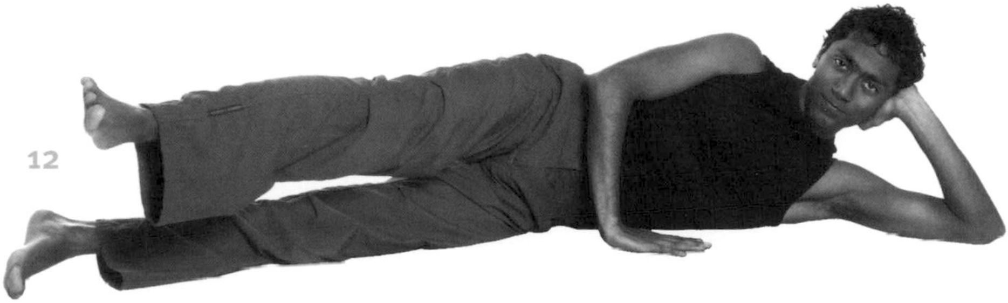

(13) With your upper leg, do ten circles clockwise
and then counterclockwise. Repeat the exercise with
the other leg and then relax.

13

(14) For the last intermediate exercise, "The Saw," sit up straight on the mat. Press your legs down as much as you can and part them slightly, stretching your arms out to the side.

14

15

(15) As you breathe in, twist your right side forward and your left side backward. Your head should be an extension of your spine and your arms and shoulders are also turned.

(16) Bend forward as you breathe out. Pull your right hand toward your left foot and stretch your left arm backward.

16

(17) Straighten up your spine again and, as you breathe in, twist to your right, keeping your back straight.

17

18

(18) As you breathe out, bend your upper body forward and reach for your right foot with your left hand and stretch your right hand back. Repeat the exercise three times on each side.

19

(19) Finish the intermediate program in the relaxation position. Lie on your back on the mat and relax.

(20) Pull your knees into your chest with your arms around your legs, pull your head toward your knees and rock back and forth along your spine.

20

# The Mind, and Soul

# Body,
# Connection

# Reduce Stress With Pilates

**The holistic idea of considering a person as a combination of mind, body, and soul is becoming more and more accepted in Western culture. Few people would now dispute the fact that all three facets influence each other. Conversely, someone who is suffering spiritually will also feel physically or mentally below par.**

In Western culture it has taken a long time for this realization to be accepted. For centuries, the body was at best considered to be a vehicle that carried us through our earthly vale of tears. Pain was God's punishment and had to be endured. One philosophical trend after another deliberately ignored the physical to look for salvation only in the spiritual.

Fortunately, times have changed. Since the 1960s, when the fitness movement started in the USA, the body has begun to receive the attention it has deserved for so long. Physical training also improves mental and spiritual well-being.

*Pilates is a holistic training method for body, mind and soul.*

In Pilates too, the occasionally very demanding exercises also focus on the body, and the Mind-Body-Soul connection developed by Joseph Pilates enables practitioners to benefit on all three levels.

However, like any sport, Pilates is not a cure-all for the cares and woes of our times. Although it is based on general physiological principles, Pilates is still a very individual training method. The benefits that can be obtained from it are dependent upon many factors, including hereditary physical conditions. That is why in Pilates you are never compared with anyone else.

*Relaxation exercises are very effective at combating stress.*

## The Body Affects the Mind and Soul

The central nervous system keeps the brain in constant contact with the rest of the body. The scientific proof of this communication was discovered by the Russian physiologist Ivan Pavlov (1849 – 1936). In his famous experiment, he placed a probe through a dog's stomach wall, to enable him to observe the changes in the animal's stomach. He noticed that production of the dog's digestive juices increased before it started to eat.

Every time he gave the dog something to eat, Pavlov rang a bell. After a while, the sound of the bell alone, which the dog now associated with food, was enough to trigger the production of the dog's digestive juices. So an abstract stimulus could cause a physical reaction. This discovery influenced psychology, as well as physiology.

Today we know that the body, mind and soul are not only connected by nerves. Some stimuli that affect our bodies, of which Pilates is one, cause very complex reactions. These include several hormonal processes.

But something else again happens when you regularly load your body. These processes were first discovered in the second half of the 20th century, and are still not fully understood. In order to understand them, we have to deal with an issue that many people going through a hard time suffer from and which is commonly misunderstood: We are talking about stress.

# Stress Doesn't Only Get on Your Nerves

The term "stress" dates back to the Canadian doctor Hans Selye (1907-1982). He developed his Adaptation Syndrome Theory (Selye's Syndrome) at the end of the 1940s. Today, we use the word stress as a synonym for anything that gets on our nerves or makes our lives difficult. However, that is only one side of the coin, for the phenomenon of stress is much more complex than that and can also be caused by positive stimuli, e.g., by extreme joy. Above all, it is a very individual matter, in which both physical and mental factors play a role.

 **TRAINING TIP**

While intensive Pilates training places the body and mind under stress, the simpler movements represent a form of active recovery, at least for the most advanced practitioners. So try to incorporate these exercises into your free time during the day. They are a valuable aid in breaking up daily stress cycles.

The important thing is not the stress-causing stimuli (stressors) that we are subjected to, but how we react to and deal with them. Many people are already stressed out if they are stopped by three red traffic lights in a row, while others are unruffled by a hectic day at work followed by their children's untidy bedroom at home. Psychologists distinguish between loading and demand. Loading represents the amount of stimulus that affects us, while

*Stressors are events, situations, people or environmental stimuli whose subjective effect causes stress.*

*Although everyone reacts differently to stress, there are a few general signs of stress common to all. These include problems of concentration and memory, anxiety, reduced self-confidence and depression.*

the demand indicates how our body reacts to this stimulus. There are many different factors that affect our reactions, including certain behavior patterns that are intended to protect us from too much stress.

## Too Much or Too Little?

The negative overtones of the word stress should not blind us to the fact that there is also a positive form of stress. Hans Selye distinguished between distress, a depressing and harmful reaction to excessive demands, and eustress, a positive and necessary activation of the body. The latter is the kind of training our bodies need to continue in order to function efficiently.

## MEDICAL TIP

**Regularly allow yourself a few quiet moments to take stock, when you work out your wishes, anxieties and hopes. If you don't want to share them with anyone else, write them down, but don't repress your needs. Instead, make concrete plans as to how to satisfy them.**

Everything would be much easier if we only had a few stimuli to cope with in life, and which we could use to our advantage. Our reactions would always be optimal. However, we have precious little control over the hectic nature of everyday life. We don't even notice most of them and therefore have no chance of guiding the stimuli in the best way. It is true that not every stress factor exceeds the critical threshold, but even the large numbers of low-level stimuli that we are confronted with leave their trace. The effects of too much stress make their presence felt in different ways, including a general reduction in well-being and the appearance of muscle problems.

*Stress can be defined as a state of alert, which prepares the body to perform at a higher level.*

The phenomenon of overtraining is well-known in sports. The term suggests that it is just a question of training too hard, when actually overtraining symptoms tend to occur when athletes in high-intensity training phases are exposed to other strong disturbing influences, e.g., in their professional or family lives.

*After a stressful day, stretching exercises can provide welcome relaxation.*

In our everyday lives, our bodies react likewise, if the load is greater than our ability to cope with it over a long period of time. Consequently, more and more people are suffering from chronic burn-out. Instead of enjoying life, they feel that their environment is increasingly dangerous. They also feel physically worn-out and lack mental resilience. Even the slightest problem during one of these stressful phases is more than enough to throw some people even deeper into crisis.

## Mental Training

The purpose of this book is not to list problems but to offer practical solutions. How can you manage to handle the negative influences that constantly surround you more effectively? One answer is to practice Pilates.

*Movement is a particularly effective weapon against stress. Dancing, going for a walk in the countryside or even doing Pilates can be a great help in reducing stress.*

We have already learned that our tolerance to stress can be improved. Extreme athletes expose themselves to situations that would give the rest of us shivers down our spines just to think about them. Peak performances certainly require a certain amount of natural ability, but a large part, which transcends the purely physical, is the result of training.

## NUTRITIONAL TIP

Make sure you consume enough folic acid and B-complex vitamins. You can find them in fresh vegetables, and they are "nerve nutrition" in the truest sense. They also render the potentially dangerous homocystein harmless. Homocystein occurs during the metabolism of certain protein connections and, according to recent findings, it is a dangerous risk factor in the appearance of heart disease.

Experienced sports psychologists know that hard physical training alone is not enough to be able to compete successfully at the highest level. Not even the most talented athlete can continue to win competitions if he is not strong enough mentally to withstand the pressure. Even hard training itself requires a great deal of stress tolerance. From a certain point of view, athletes have an advantage compared to "normal" people. They can usually rely on their entourage, who relieve them of many mundane problems. This naturally reduces the amount of stressors.

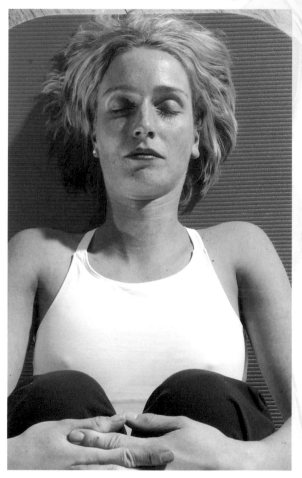

However, the pressure that elite athletes are under is enormous. How do they manage to cope with it and still improve their performances? They do it with the help of mental training. That may sound rather odd at first, but it is really not that complicated.

There are essentially two factors: the mental concentration on certain recurring movements and visualization of them. This is already familiar to us in the Pilates system, since concentration and visualization are among the core

*Mental training can mobilize hidden powers and remove mental blocks.*

*First try to diagnose negative thinking patterns and then to replace them with positive ones. Prepare yourself for situations and events by imagining positive outcomes.*

elements of the training method. Joseph Pilates had already started using these factors long before sports psychologists and motivational gurus did.

What help do concentration and visualization provide on the psychological and spiritual levels in the fight against stress? How do they help us to become more resilient and therefore perform more efficiently? While on the physical side they help us do the exercises more effectively, concentration and visualization also help us to do something that in our culture is being pushed more and more into the background: They force us to be in the here and now. Physically, we are there all the time, but just think how often your thoughts wander during the day. In addition to being inundated by external stimuli, we are also constantly burdening ourselves with things that either lie behind us in the past or have not yet happened. Many people forget that the future arises from the active structuring of the present.

 ——— **TRAINING TIP** ———

**Beginners in particular need to be calm and comfortable in order to learn concentration and visualization techniques. If you practice at home, you should start by doing it alone in a quiet, warm room wearing comfortable sports clothes. Later, you will be able to concentrate even in a noisy room full of people.**

How many people sit in the office thinking about what they are going to have for dinner and possible problems with their partner or loneliness waiting for them at home.

Thinking about problems and situations that we cannot do anything about at the time makes our blood pressure shoot up, as our subconscious cannot distinguish between reality and fiction. This anticipation is completely unnecessary and it also prevents us from concentrating on what we should actually be doing at the time. As this makes you take longer to do your work, it can actually create new stress factors.

*Visualization exercises with beautiful images and fantasies can have a very restful and relaxing effect.*

Psychoregulation, achieved by doing regular concentration and visualization exercises, helps you turn stressful conditions to your advantage. The ability to concentrate totally on the Pilates exercises also has a positive effect on other areas of your life over time. It helps to reduce unnecessary mental stress and to deal with existing stress much more effectively.

# Exercises

The following exercises enable you to train the conscious perception of the mind, body, and soul connection. They are graded according to difficulty: medium (◉◉) and difficult (◉◉◉).

## Double Leg Kick ◉◉

**1**

(1) Lie on your stomach on the mat. Clasp your hands together behind your back with your palms facing upward. Turn your head to the right. As you breathe in, kick your heels three times against your bottom, as you contract your gluteal muscles strongly. Your hips should remain on the floor.

**2**

(2) Next stretch your arms right back and raise your upper body from the floor as you pull your abdominal muscles in. Lower your upper body and turn your head to the left this time. Repeat the whole movement sequence three times.

(1) Lie on your stomach on the mat. Place your hands underneath your shoulders and rest on your toes.

**1**

(2) As you breathe out, raise yourself up into the push-up position.

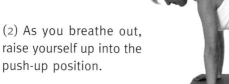

**2**

**3**

(3) As you breathe in, raise one leg until it is level with your bottom, keeping it straight. As you breathe out, lower the leg again.

(4) Repeat the exercise with the other leg. Keep your hips and the Box straight. Repeat this exercise, which requires well-trained back and abdominal muscles, three to five times with each leg.

**4**

## THE IMPORTANCE OF FEAR

Fear is a factor that has a noticeable influence on our state of excitement, and which we are all subject to in our lives. Compared to adults, babies are relatively brave – they come into the world with only a few basic fears, e.g., of loud noises. Most fears that shape our later life are learned over the years. Some fears are connected to certain objects or situations. They prevent us from taking unnecessary or uncalculated risks.

In childhood, we learn mainly by painful personal experience. It doesn't matter how many times a mother tells her child not to touch the oven door because it is hot; the child only takes notice once she has burned her fingers on it. When we are older, our brains are able to add the warnings of others to the lessons of our own experiences. We don't have to jump out of a third-floor window to know that we could hurt ourselves very badly if we do.

These real anxieties make up only part of the fears that are constantly present in our heads. Several anxieties have no concrete cause. Many people are afraid of the future, although they live in a secure environment. Others are terrified of the slightest noise in the dark, even though there is no one around.

Pilates can also be a great help in cases like these. Discipline and control are important factors in combating fear. While the loss of control leads to insecurity, the feeling of being in control provides security. Consequently, by helping you to control your body, Pilates enables you to control your thoughts and feelings.

## SUMMARY

- There is an ongoing reciprocal influence between body, mind and soul.

- Constant over-stimulation makes life hard to cope with.

- Every person reacts differently to stress.

- There are several exercises that can improve your stress tolerance.

- Concentration and visualization can manage stimulation, taking it to the optimum level.

# Advanced Program

When you have mastered the basic (pages 68 – 73) and intermediate exercises (pages 114 – 119), you can move on to this advanced exercise routine, but only do so when your body awareness has reached a very good level.

**1**

(1) Pull your navel toward your spine to activate your powerhouse.

**2**

(2) Start the exercise program with the "Roll Over." Lie on the floor on your back and raise your straight legs until they are vertical.

(3) Using the strength of your powerhouse, raise your hips and let your legs fall toward your head. Press the palms of your hands against the floor.

**3**

(4) Roll backward until only your shoulders are lying on the mat. Separate your legs to should-width apart. Then close your legs and as your breathe in, roll back under control to the starting position. Repeat the exercise five times and relax.

**4**

(5) "The Teaser" requires a very strong powerhouse. Lie on your back, bend your knees and stretch your arms behind you.

(6) Extend your legs diagonally upward.

(7) Raise your arms, head and shoulders and then roll your whole spine off the floor.

(8) Bring your arms forward and breathe calmly as you hold this position. Round your back and then roll back to the starting position. Repeat the exercise five times and then relax.

9

(9) Lie on your stomach to prepare for the "Swimming Position." Stretch your arms in front of you shoulder-width apart, raise your head slightly and keep looking at the floor.

10

(10) As you breathe out, simultaneously raise your right arm and left leg slightly from the floor. Keep your head in line with your spine.

11

(11) Now, raise your left leg and your right arm and repeat the raising and lowering of your opposite arms and legs twenty times. Then sit on your heels, place your forehead on the floor and relax in this Relaxation Position (see figure 21).

(12) Lie on your stomach again for "The Swan." Place your hands underneath your shoulders and keep your elbows next to your sides.

12

(13) Activate your back muscles and breathe out as you straighten your arms.

13

(14) Bring your arms forward and roll your upper body forward. Keep your legs straight as they swing upward.

14

(15) Lower your legs and simultaneously pull your upper body upward. Repeat the rocking movement five times, then sit on your heels, place your forehead on the floor and relax in the Relaxation Position (see figure 21).

15

## *EXERCISE ROUTINE*

**16**

(17) Stretch the left side of your body by pulling your left arm over to the right as you breathe out. Then straighten up as you breathe in.

**17**

(16) Sit on your heels in the starting position for "The Mermaid." Sit to the left of your heels. Hold your ankles with your right hand and raise your left arm vertically upward.

**18**

(18) Now support yourself by placing your left hand on the floor. Pull your right arm up and then over to the left to stretch your right side. Repeat the whole exercise five times.

(19) The exercise routine finishes with "Relaxing." Sit on your heels on the mat.

(20) Round your back and let your upper body slide onto the floor. Stretch your arms in front of you.

(21) Bring your arms back and place your hands next to your feet. Take a few deep breaths and relax in this position.

(22) Then roll your spine up vertebra by vertebra until you are sitting on your heels again.

# Photo & Illustration Credits

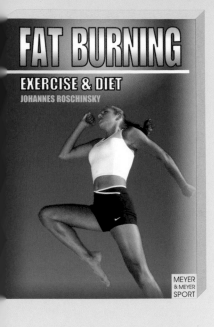

Johannes Roschinsky
## Fat Burning
### Exercise & Diet

A theoretical introduction to the topics of bodyweight and nutrition is accompanied by descriptions and comparisons of various endurance sports and tips given for effective training. Fat Burning is the guidebook for all those who want to achieve lasting weight-loss by eating a healthy diet and exercising regularly.

192 pages, full-color print
112 color photos
Paperback, 5$^3$/4" x 8$^1$/4"
ISBN: 1-84126-140-8
£ 12.95 UK/$ 17.95 US
$ 25.95 CDN/€ 16.90

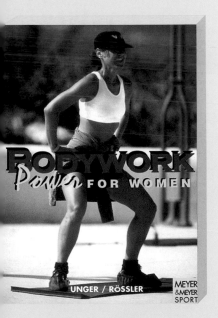

Edgar Unger & Jürgen Rößler
## Bodywork
### Power for Women

This book provides a comprehensive program and detailed workout instructions so that you can change your figure according to the goals you set yourself, stay younger in a biological way – and healthier. It also helps to arrest a decline in sporting activity and suggests how to improve fitness through a variety of exercises and training programs in the illustrated training section.

144 pages, 76 figures
Paperback, 5$^3$/4" x 8$^1$/4"
ISBN 1-84126-022-3
£ 12.95 UK/$ 17.95 US
$ 25.95 CDN/€ 16.90

MEYER & MEYER Sport | sales@m-m-sports.com | www.m-m-sports.com

MEYER &MEYER SPORT

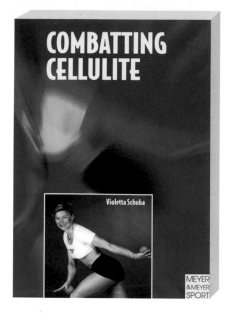

Violetta Schuba
## Combatting Cellulite

This book offers a wide-ranging, practice-oriented endurance and muscle training program alongside background information about building up one's skin how cellulite starts and about diet. It is directed at interested amateurs, at those who are affected themselves, as well as at trainers and fitness training instructors.

152 pages, two-color print
77 photos, 25 illustrations
Paperback, 5$\,^3/4$" x 8$\,^1/4$"
ISBN 1-84126-032-0
£ 9.95 UK/$ 14.95 US
$ 20.95 CDN/€ 16.90

Monika Mildenberger-Schneider
## Fit 4 Ever – Strength Training

Older generations are often into sport for health reasons. Muscle power training is then a must, particularly in view of the age-associated changes in muscle structure. The training described uses simple aids that are either available in the home or can be purchased at an affordable price.

136 pages, two-color print
237 photos
Paperback, 5$\,^3/4$" x 8$\,^1/4$"
ISBN 1-84126-129-7
£ 9.95 UK/$ 14.95 US
$ 20.95 CDN/€ 14.90

MEYER & MEYER Sport | sales@m-m-sports.com | www.m-m-sports.com

MEYER
&MEYER
SPORT